WASHINGTON, D.C.

by James Playsted Wood

drawings by Joseph Papin

THE SEABURY PRESS · NEW YORK

Washington, D.C.

Second Printing, 1967

Text Copyright © 1966 by James Playsted Wood
Art Copyright © 1966 by Joseph Papin

Library of Congress Catalog Card Number 66-16654

529-467-C-7.5-5
Printed in the United States of America

For Frances and D. Norman Craig
FROM JAMES PLAYSTED WOOD

and

For Jane
FROM JOSEPH PAPIN

WASHINGTON, D.C.

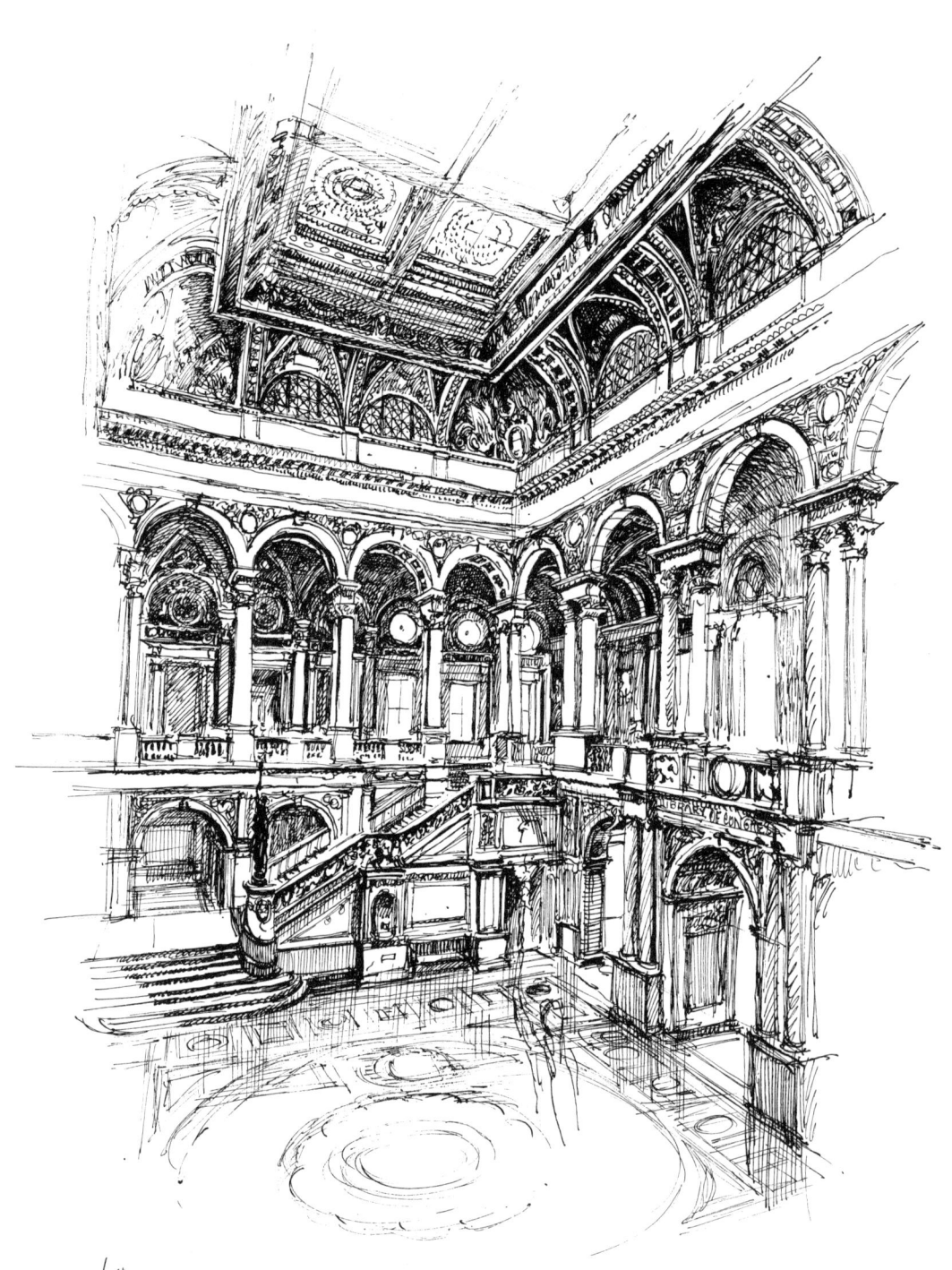

Stairway Main Hall
Library of Congress

1

W<small>ASHINGTON</small> is wonderful. That will be the conclusion of this look at the capital of the United States which has become the capital of the Western World, and there is no point in keeping it a secret. It can't be kept secret, for it will show on every page, just as it shows in Washington itself. Washington is wonderful. It is filled with wonders which arouse wonder.

Usually there are just three possibilities. Something is just the way you think it is, or it is completely different from what you think it is, or it is somewhere in between. This would be true if Washington were any other city, but Washington is not any other city. It is Washington, and because it is Washington it is probably all three and several other things besides.

Washington is sign and symbol. It was founded to signalize the advent of a new nation that was a new kind of nation, a republic in which men of their own free will and by their own actions governed themselves. It is idea, the democratic idea that Abraham Lincoln defined many troubled years later when he called it government of the people, by the people, for the people. It is dream, the dream that in this way men pursuing happiness can arrive safely at their destination.

At the same time, Washington is the intricately and awesomely complex machinery that operates a great country. It makes our laws, interprets them, enforces them. It determines our relations with the rest of the world, determines whether we are at war or at peace. It directs us in the fighting of our wars, in our explorations of space, in our plumbing of the sea, in our treatment of each other. Increasingly, it takes care of us in more and more departments of our communal and personal lives.

Washington is beautiful. Whatever else Washington is or is not, it is beautiful, one of the most beautiful cities in the world.

Washington has stately embassies and glittering used car lots. It has the White House and colossal, moderately stupendous, super-gigantic bargain sales on Washington's Birthday. It has the Capitol and splendid hotels and Rock Creek Park and Capitol Transit buses and the Lincoln Memorial and Peoples Drug Stores and handsome Foxhall Road. It has Georgetown University, George Washington University, American University, Howard University, the University of Maryland just outside, and Hot Shoppe restaurants all over the place. It has a new Senate Office Building, which cost millions piled on millions of dollars, and it has old men fishing quietly on the banks of the Potomac.

Washington has Japanese cherry trees, azaleas, camellias, Judas trees, about 270,000 federal government employes, and it is the hottest hotbed of gossip in the United States. As long ago as 1907, Henry James called Washington "The City of Conversation" and said that this

converse had just one subject. "Washington talks about herself, and about almost nothing else." It still does.

The Site

George Washington never lived in Washington. John Adams was the first President to live in the White House. George Washington did choose the site of the city and the sites of the Capitol and what was then called "The President's Palace," the White House.

In June 1783, Pennsylvania veterans of the Revolution marched on the State House in Philadelphia, where the Declaration of Independence had been signed and where Congress was meeting. Not unreasonably, these soldiers of a victorious army wanted to be paid. Prudently, Congress locked itself in the building and the insistent veterans outside. There was some shouting and some name-calling. As soon as it was safe to go out, Congress fled and took up quarters in Princeton,

New Jersey. What it wanted most now was to be outside the jurisdiction of any state, thus safe from recurrence of such unpleasantness.

When George Washington was inaugurated first President of the new United States on April 30, 1789, he took the oath of office on Wall Street at New York City Hall, which Major Pierre Charles L'Enfant had redesigned for the use of Congress. New York was not to remain the capital for long.

Having been harried from place to place, Congress was uneasy. While in session in Princeton, it had decided that for safety and comfort it would meet alternately in two places. There would be two capitals: one on the Delaware, one in Maryland. Congress would hold one session at Trenton, the next at Annapolis.

Article I, Section 8, Paragraph 17 of the Constitution adopted in 1787 halved this political ambition. It provided for the creation of a Federal District, not to exceed ten miles square, that should be the one

WASHINGTON, D.C.

permanent seat of the United States government. There followed long and loud debate as to where this Federal District should be. Senators and Representatives, then as now, wanted what would do them and their constituents the most good.

Two Virginia gentlemen, George Washington and Thomas Jefferson, advocated the location at or near the lower falls of the Potomac, which Congress had already designated as one possibility. For one thing, this place was central, north and south. As all of the original states were along the Atlantic seaboard, the question of centrality east and west seemed unimportant. By this time, Congress wanted Baltimore.

With the help of Alexander Hamilton, Washington and Jefferson got their way. Hamilton as Secretary of the Treasury wanted the federal government to assume the war debts of the individual states. He would use his influence to sway Congress to the Potomac site if Jefferson would back his financial proposal. The deal was made. Jefferson backed Hamilton, and July 1, 1790, the Senate voted 14 to 12 for a Potomac River site between the mouth of the Eastern Branch and the Connogochegue, 20 miles south of the Pennsylvania line. By a vote of 32 to 29 the House of Representatives agreed.

When President Washington himself went to pick the actual spot, he was met by suitably arrayed and probably quite excited landowners

on horseback. There were fitting ceremonies. Some of the farm and plantation owners scented profit. Some were reluctant to give up any of their land. A few may have visualized the possibilities and fully realized the import of the occasion.

Most cities just happen. They grow up about a seaport, a ferry landing on a river, a mill, a highway, or a spot where a group of people have sought refuge from conditions in some other place. Washington, District of Columbia, was on purpose. It was deliberately placed and carefully planned.

The region had one great attraction for George Washington. He was tired of riding on or behind a horse. After the great distances he had covered in his military campaigns and as the first Mr. President, he was glad to find a spot and to found a seat of government not too far from his beloved "Mount Vernon." Before he left, he chose a ten-mile square of marshy land on both sides of the Potomac River for the capital.

This was wilderness land and farmland, but it was in a long-settled and fairly wealthy part of the country. John Smith had come within ten miles of it in 1608. About 1650, Scots and Irish had settled along the river's banks. In 1662, Lord Baltimore granted lands to a George Thompson who brought in more Scottish settlers. They built substantial houses, each man naming his tract in what was known as the New Scotland Hundred. Among these plantations were "Argyle," "Allinson's Forest," "Rock of Dumbarton," "Fife Large." Humbler citizens chose names descriptive of their smaller holdings or their attitudes toward life. Some sounded like the names of California mining claims two centuries later: "Widow's Mite," "Plain Dealing," "Little Chance."

After President Washington had decided on the location, Virginia and Maryland condemned the farm and plantation lands selected for the new capital, and Washington persuaded the landholders to convey the ground to the United States. Owners were paid nothing for land designated for the erection of public buildings and about $67.00 an acre for the rest of the land they deeded over. The landowners retained half their lots for speculation—for sale to the highest bidders.

Most of the landowners were agreeable. The biggest of them was

WASHINGTON, D.C.

not. James Burnes, who had had a small plantation of about six hundred acres but had come to own most of the land on the Maryland side from what is now about 17th Street and Constitution Avenue to the border of Georgetown, held out for large profits. Washington demurred. So did Burnes. Washington accused Burnes of obstinacy. The story has been branded untrue, but Burnes is said to have retorted, "Aye, mon! An' had ye no married the Widow Custis . . . you'd a been a surveyor the day—an' a michty poor ane!" Washington eventually got his land, and Burnes eventually made a fortune from his large acreage.

On January 24, 1791, the District of Columbia was proclaimed the official site of the capital of the United States. Congress would sit in Philadelphia until the new capital was ready. Three commissioners were appointed for the District: Thomas Jefferson, Daniel Carroll, and Dr. David Stuart. L'Enfant was appointed to plan the city, and Washington returned to meet him there so that they could go over the ground together.

L'Enfant

Born in 1754, Pierre Charles L'Enfant was the son of a court painter in France. After some training as an engineer and architect, he

WASHINGTON, D.C.

had come to America at the age of 23 to fight in the Revolution. Commissioned a lieutenant of engineers, December 1, 1776, he spent the cold winter at Valley Forge. Two years later, he was wounded leading an assault on Savannah. Taken prisoner at Charleston, he was not exchanged until 1782 when he was promoted to major by special act of Congress and awarded a pension by his native France. At Lafayette's request, Washington had sat to L'Enfant for his portrait, but this was finished in outline only and even the outline has not survived. He designed the insignia of the Society of the Cincinnati, an order founded by the officers of the disbanding Continental Army, and was sent to France by Washington to have the design executed. Gifted and

imaginative, L'Enfant was impractical even then and soon ran into financial difficulties.

When he and Washington rode over the Potomac ground together, L'Enfant was enchanted by what he saw, but even more enchanted by

16

WASHINGTON, D.C.

his vision of what the proposed federal city might become. He drew on his knowledge of cities and capitals he knew—Versailles, London, Paris, Philadelphia, Williamsburg, Annapolis—but even more on what he envisioned. Deeply influenced by the grandeur of Versailles, which he had known as a boy and young man, he conceived the idea of a long mall, or boulevard, and of avenues radiating from a central point.

L'Enfant drew up his plans eagerly, with great imagination and no regard for expense or practicality. He planned his mall to extend a mile and a half from the Capitol to the Presidential Palace in which he wished to combine "the sumptuousness of a palace and the agreeableness of a country seat." He planned avenues 160 feet wide and streets 89 feet wide. On Jenkins' Hill, which Washington had chosen as site of the legislative halls, he planned a Capitol which would show the world the beauty and grandeur of the republican ideal.

The Beginnings

Andrew Ellicott, the Pennsylvania surveyor hired to lay out the new District, was not as impressed as L'Enfant. He wrote his wife that the site would not compare to Philadelphia or Germantown, but he went briskly about his business. He began to cut a 40-foot path through the woods along each side of the Federal District. The first two-foot-high milepost was set up at Alexandria, Virginia, with Masonic ceremonies, March 15, 1791.

The District was a square, each side ten miles in length, with the point of the top right angle pointing north. It took in two already-flourishing towns. On the Virginia side of the Potomac, Alexandria (which had been Bell Haven) had stately homes and formal gardens. General Braddock had dined there with the ladies before he went out—young George Washington with him—to take the Indians, who took him instead. Georgetown, on the northern shore of the river, west of the planned President's Palace, had its stately homes too. It prospered from the tobacco and fur trade. It had sent two companies of militia to Boston immediately on the outbreak of the Revolution, supplied with armament from its Foxhall Foundry. Its women had given their household treasures to the Continental cause; one of them, it is said, gave an apronful of gold.

The Maryland *Journal,* September 30, 1791, carried a lyrical real estate advertisement. In two weeks the first sale of lots in the Federal District would take place. The newspaper praised the development highly:

> The plan was designed and drawn by the celebrated Major L'Enfant, and is an inconceivable improvment upon all other cities in the world, combining not only convenience, regularity, elegance of prospect, and a free circulation of air, but everything grand and beautiful that can possibly be introduced into a city . . . the plans not only produce amazement in Europe, but meet the admiration of all future ages.

The blurb writer was more enthusiastic than the bidders. The lots sold slowly. L'Enfant was not disturbed. He went ahead rapturously with his grand plan, so rapturously and extravagantly that he was soon under attack. The commissioners resented his high-handed tactics. George Washington cautioned L'Enfant and tried to reestablish peace between him and the commissioners. He failed. In late February 1792, L'Enfant demanded dismissal of the commissioners, and that he be allowed to act independently in making a structural reality of his plans. Instead, Congress accepted his resignation.

Embittered, L'Enfant left Washington. He declined a professorship at the United States Military Academy at West Point. He tried this and that, returned miserably to the Washington that was his dream, and, after being looked after by a charitable friend in Silver Spring in Maryland just north of Washington, died virtually a pauper. In 1909, his body was disinterred, laid in state at the Capitol, and then placed in a Grecian tomb in the Arlington National Cemetery.

The wealthy and cultured of the country were comfortable in Boston, New York, and especially Philadelphia. These were already old and well-established cities where polite society dined on damask

WASHINGTON, D.C.

with fine china and silver, read books, listened to music, went to the theater, and conversed learnedly or charmingly. Washington offered no such amenities. It was only a possibility, a place of castles in the air with no foundations under them and of slaves' and laborers' shanties which did not aspire to be castles at all.

President Washington urged all possible speed in the building of the city that had been named for him. With Jefferson and Madison he attended the sale of lots. He forecast a profitable commercial future for the city. He had a house built as a speculation on North Capitol Street and bought a lottery ticket on Washington's first hotel, which was being built by Samuel Blodgett, the District's first Supervisor of Buildings.

As a speculation, James Greenleaf of Massachusetts bought 3,000 lots from the commissioners. The country's richest man, Robert Morris of Philadelphia, financier of the Revolution, joined forces with Greenleaf, and they got the land cheaply on the promise to build ten houses a year. They went bankrupt, and Morris went to debtor's prison for a term. He died broken and nearly forgotten. Washington, D.C. did him in as it had done in L'Enfant.

The White House, the President's Palace, was the first public building to get under way in Washington. A competition was held for the best plan. Thomas Jefferson competed but lost. The prize of $500 went to James Hoban of South Carolina. No architect, but a gentleman amateur, Hoban, who was Irish born, drew on the Duke of Leinster's house in Dublin, the Vice Regal Lodge, and on his ideal of the southern plantation manor facing a broad park and a river.

The cornerstone of the White House was laid with elaborate ceremony on Columbus Day 1792, just three hundred years after Columbus discovered America. Work was begun immediately, with many disputes between Stephen Halleck, runner-up in the competition and a practising architect on the job, and James Hoban. George Washington chivvied the work along, but it went slowly, for the palace and country seat was being built to last. Its walls were of brick laid to a thickness of four feet, and these were faced with gray Virginia sandstone.

WASHINGTON, D.C.

The prize of $500 (which the commissioners had to borrow from Samuel Blodgett) for the best design for the Capitol went to Dr. William Thornton. Thornton, like Alexander Hamilton a native of the West Indies, was a physician, but though he had studied medicine at Edinburgh and Abderdeen, he did not practice. Instead, he occupied himself with travel and artistic interests. He had designed the handsome building of the Library Company of Philadelphia in 1789.

George Washington was present when the cornerstone of the Capitol was laid September 18, 1793. Masonic lodges paraded in full regalia. There were two bands. Companies of Virginia Artillery boomed off their cannon with enthusiasm. A 500-pound ox was roasted whole, and an army of workmen soon descended on Capitol Hill with shovels, trowels, saws, and hammers. Halleck was in charge of construction

here, too. Once more he had great fault to find with an amateur's design, but the sawing and hammering and shouting went on, and the Capitol began to rise.

Washington urged importing workmen to hasten the reality of the city. He was heeded, and the men brought in to work lived anywhere they could, in the few houses the village already had or in hastily erected shacks. There was a wealth of plans. There were some three thousand people in the straggling river village. There was ambition and determination enough. What was lacking was money.

This hardly deterred the planners. Regularly there was the shrill tootling of fifes and the brave thumping of drums as small bands of men in Masonic aprons—George Washington was a serious Mason—marched solemnly through woods, swamps, and streams to lay the cornerstone of one projected government building here and another there, on avenues that still existed only on L'Enfant's plan.

The Government

By 1800 there was hardly a city; but there was enough for a start, and the United States government moved to Washington. There were now 109 brick homes, 253 wooden ones, and two rows of houses built by speculators on the river side of the White House, but there were still more fields and brushland than city streets. Five miles down the Potomac was the port of Alexandria with its beautiful pre-Revolutionary homes, but Washington still had only a few ornate mansions and many squalid dwellings. Many of the newcomers were horrified by what they saw as a "mudhole," a "backwoods settlement in the wilderness," a "city of streets without houses." These were some of the more polite terms they used to describe their new home and office.

The fable is that the entire federal government arrived in a sloop that sailed down the Delaware from Philadelphia, across the Chesapeake and up the Potomac. Perhaps the sloop brought the government's records and a few clerks. It could not have carried all who came. By this time, the expanding national government had 131 office-

WASHINGTON, D.C.

holders, and everybody, the President and Mrs. Adams, Senators, Congressmen, and clerks, had their goods and chattels. Finding a place to put themselves and their belongings was the first problem.

The White House was unfinished. Most of it was still unplastered. Abigail Adams hung her washing in the East Room, the grand ballroom of the palace. The White House was damp and cold, and for some reason, firewood to warm it was unobtainable. The Adamses shivered.

The Vice President did better for himself. Thomas Jefferson got two warm rooms in a tavern. He had a whole sitting room to himself and a whole bedroom. Most members of the government, high-ranking officers as well as the more lowly, had to share their quarters, even their beds, with their fellows, in what was now officially the Capital of the United States.

If members of the government were horrified, the diplomats from other nations, who, perforce, had to give up their comfortable quarters in Philadelphia and follow to Washington, shuddered convulsively. Bad enough to be exiled from civilized Europe to the savage Western Hemisphere, but this! This, they assured each other, was the uncivilized end, and there was at first little to persuade them otherwise.

Conditions, as they usually do, improved. There was good hunting in the marshes. There was polite society in Alexandria and in Georgetown, and there were the beginnings of a social season in Washington with visiting and leaving cards. Ladies and gentlemen went abroad, despite the bad roads and streets, in their carriages behind smartly groomed horses, a coachman on the box, perhaps a liveried servant seated behind. A few plays were put on by companies adventuring out of Philadelphia. Between May and November, the U.S. Marine Band played on the White House grounds. There were even books; the wealthy had their own and the Library of Congress already wallowed in an appropriation of $1,000 a year.

There was one thing even better than all this. When the Jockey Club held its annual meeting on a field north of the town, Congress stopped talking and went to the races. Congressmen went. The President went. Schools were closed, and society ladies in their carriages, ambassadors in theirs, laborers, Negro slaves, everybody went, and an uproarious time was had by all. The crowd not only entered gleefully into the betting, drinking, shouting, and quarreling, but also everybody who could took part. After the regular races were over, Senators and Cabinet members, farmers, traders, slaves jumped into whatever rigs they had or could obtain and drove full speed around the course.

When Jefferson, who built the colonnades and laid out the grounds, was President, Indian squaws dressed in flowing calico skirts came to the White House receptions. Painted Sac and Osage chiefs came to confer with him. In cages out on the lawn were the grizzly bears which Meriwether Lewis had sent back from his travels as a gift to his chief.

Yet it was not all Indians and grizzly bears, not all uncouth, for Dolly Madison was there now. The black-haired young widow Senator Aaron Burr had introduced to Congressman James Madison in Philadelphia became queen of Washington society when, her husband now Secretary of State, she was made official White House hostess under Jefferson, who was a widower. Both elegant and friendly, she presided at White House balls and receptions while Jefferson was President, and then during her husband's two-term administration.

Men of wit and intelligence and women of culture began to be attracted to Washington now by its growing cosmopolitan society. Precedence at dinner became a matter of national and international importance as Dolly Madison glorified the tradition of entertaining that had been strong in Washington from its village days and is strong there today.

Many people in Washington are visitors, at least transients. This was true in the early 1800s, through most of the last century, and, where officeholders and their families are concerned, is still true. A Representative serves for only two years before he must be reelected or vanish from the Washington scene. A President serves only twice that long, and even Senators can be certain only of the six years for which they are elected. The permanent homes of politicians are elsewhere.

In the early days of the country, Congressmen and Cabinet members often lived in rented rooms, apartments, or, if they were affluent enough to bring their families to Washington with them and fortunate enough to find a place, in leased houses. Most of the permanent residents of the city were from the hospitable South. They felt that it was up to them to entertain these temporary incumbents of important and unimportant offices, and they did. Washingtonians still do.

For more than a dozen years Dolly Madison laughed and talked and put polished ambassadors and raw frontier Congressmen at ease at White House social functions. Her purple hat with its white plumes dazzled everywhere. At her husband's first inaugural ball, the most elaborate Washington had seen to that time, Dolly wore a turban with bird of paradise feathers. Even the rather plain and not overly social Thomas Jefferson, who retired that night to his vast and vastly debt-ridden estate "Monticello," not far from Charlottesville, enjoyed himself.

War of 1812

Washington thrives on war. The city really came into its own as the beleaguered headquarters of the Union during the Civil War. It responded to its first international challenge in World War I by great expansion. It had 38,000 federal employes in 1917, but 111,000 by the fall of 1918; and Washington did not fall away after that first world conflict but continued to grow. It experienced another thrust forward in international importance during and immediately after World War II and responded with further accelerated growth, but Washington did not thrive during the first war it experienced. When war with England was declared in June of 1812, there was tremendous excitement in the capital—a great display of military force and ardor on the declaration of "Mr. Madison's War." All District of Columbia males of military age were subject to service in the militia, which paraded handsomely at the second Madison inauguration.

The war came nearer. The British fleet blockaded Chesapeake Bay. The enemy pillaged and burned Havre de Grace. In July 1813,

*Octagon House
18th and New York ave.
one of Washington's most
historic houses. Excellent
example of Late Georgian design
built by William Thornton, original
architect of the Capitol, completed in 1800.
President Madison took refuge and
residence there for about a year in 1814
after the British burned the White House.*

British men-o'-war sailed up the Potomac to within 60 miles of the city. Fortifications were hastily bolstered. The militia marched and made warlike gestures. There were frightening rumors of a slave uprising. In June 1814, British landing parties reached shore only 22 miles from Washington. The militia rushed out to find the invaders, but somehow missed them.

By late August 1814, the British forces were almost on Washington. Women, children, servants, and clerks fled the city carrying all the personal and government property they could to safety. Carrying Gilbert Stuart's portrait of Washington, which now hangs in the East Room of the White House, and important state papers, Dolly Madison left in her carriage on the hot afternoon of August 24. After 8 men had

WASHINGTON, D.C.

been killed and 11 wounded, the militia fled too. The British entered the city unopposed.

Admiral Sir George Cockburn and his men swarmed into the Capitol. Enthroning himself in the Speaker's chair in the House of Representatives, the admiral posed a rhetorical question. "Gentlemen, the question is, shall this harbor of Yankee democracy be burned? All in favor will say aye." There was not a single nay.

Using books from the Library of Congress as torches, the British fired every public building they could find. They burned the Capitol, the White House, the Potomac Bridge, the War and Treasury Buildings, and the arsenal at Greenleaf Point. They even set fire to the house George Washington had built. Seemingly, they did not like him. Only the Post Office escaped. The only British casualties were about one hundred men whom their fellows, in their happy enthusiasm, blew up along with the arsenal.

A severe storm helped the invaders. A high wind blew the roofs

WASHINGTON, D.C.

off houses and helped spread the raging flames. The storm also helped the Americans. The heavy rains that came in with the gale winds helped put out the fires. Once sure that the conflagration and the storm had done all the damage they could, the conquerors moved merrily on to Alexandria where the pickings were better. They sacked the city and loaded their ships with cotton, tobacco, sugar, and wines.

Washington was a smoking ruin when the President and his wife, the politicians, the women, children, and servants dribbled back into the city four days later. The White House was a burned-out shell. The dome of the Capitol and both wings were in ashes. The Treasury and the War Department were gone. The Navy Yard at Anacostia and the Greenleaf Point Arsenal were rubble.

It seemed unlikely the city could be rebuilt. Philadelphia hopefully offered to take in the homeless Congress. So, competitively, did other cities. Stubbornly, the House decided to remain in ruined Washington. So did the Senate. Federal departments found shelter wher-

ever they could, mostly in private homes. The banks lent money for rebuilding. The Madisons moved into the Octagon House on New York Avenue. Jefferson helped rebuild the Library of Congress by selling it most of his library of some ten thousand volumes for $25,000, and the books were carted in from "Monticello." Jefferson, in financial straits, was glad of the money.

Urged on by Dolly Madison, James Hoban began the restoration of the White House. Benjamin Latrobe, who had designed the Hall of Representatives after Jefferson appointed him Surveyor of Public Buildings, helped with the rebuilding of the gutted Capitol. Stonecutters, bricklayers, and carpenters were brought in from other cities. It might still lack sanitation. Water might still come from corner pumps. It would be years before all the millions of dollars worth of property and the years of human effort could be replaced, but this time Washington was doggedly determined. It meant to stay.

2

I<small>N</small> December 1962, President Kennedy gave a dinner to honor the Nobel Prize Winners of the Western Hemisphere. In welcoming them he said, "I think this is the most extraordinary collection of talent, of human knowledge, that has ever been gathered together at the White House, with the possible exception of when Thomas Jefferson dined alone."

Of all our Presidents, the gifted and versatile Jefferson, who was scientist, lawyer, architect, and classical scholar, as well as the author of the Declaration of Independence, is generally considered to have been the most learned. Certainly he was among the wisest. He thought and wrote on many subjects. He studied government deeply and came to a conclusion: That government is best which governs least.

WASHINGTON, D.C.

The American people have reversed Jefferson's decision. Through their votes, the majority have made it clear that they believe that government is best which governs most.

We expect the federal government to do those things for us that men once expected to do for themselves or to have done under state or local control. We look to the federal government for education, medical care, financial grants to states and cities, unemployment pay, pensions, social security, urban renewal, flood control, and scores of other services. As the United States has changed from the simple republic Thomas Jefferson knew to a socialized democracy and the leader among the nations of the western world, the federal government has grown in size and power until it is the nation's largest single industry. As the seat of this government, Washington has grown with it.

For many years the Jeffersonian philosophy of government prevailed. Americans were busy about other matters. Their energy went into conquering the wilderness and developing a continent; into agriculture, business, and industry. The national government was sometimes little more than a convenient association of sovereign states, each jealous of its rights. It was in New York, Boston, Philadelphia, then Chicago and cities to the north and west that industry and commerce centered. These were the places that flourished as the country farmed, mined, built its railroads and its factories, and as ambitious and fortunate men built the great fortunes of the nineteenth century. Government mattered less than getting things done, and for a long time Washington remained little more than a unique and uniquely pretentious village.

When the American historian Henry Adams first saw it in 1850, the boy from Quincy and Boston whose grandfather and great-grandfather had both been Presidents, found it a southern village. Wheel tracks wandered down dirt streets past low wooden buildings and houses. Here and there, the Treasury, the Patent Office, the Post Office faced each other, in his words, like "white Greek temples in the abandoned gravel pits of a deserted Syrian city." Jefferson's grizzly bears were gone, but President Zachary Taylor's charger, "Whitey," grazed placidly on the White House lawn. Man and horse were heroes of the

WASHINGTON, D.C.

Mexican War, and the Adams boy met them both. In 1860, just before the outbreak of the Civil War, Adams found Washington "the same rude colony camped in the same forest with the same unfinished Greek temples for workrooms and the same sloughs for roads" that it had been in 1850, or, he thought, even in 1800. The nation's capital city had changed little in more than a half century.

Henry Adams, who returned from the American embassy in London after the close of the Civil War and chose to live in Washington where he remained most of the time until his death in 1918, should see Washington now.

When the United States government moved from Philadelphia to Washington in 1800, the country of 20 states had a total population of 5,308,483. Federal officeholders in the District of Columbia totaled 131. There are more than 131 government employes in Washington now. For a country of 50 states and over 190,000,000 population, when all types of government, national, state, and local, are combined, we

now have almost twice as many people working for government as the total population of the country in 1800. At last count, the country had 9,840,000 men and women in government employ. Of this number, 2,491,791 work for the federal government—not including the Central Intelligence Agency and the National Security Agency, whose numbers are as secret as their activities. This is a number far larger than the total population of many of the states.

In Washington alone there are 294,000 government employes: 264,000 work for the national government and 30,000 for the District of Columbia. The actual figure for the number of federal government employes in the whole Washington Metropolitan area is larger, for some huge installations like the Pentagon are in Virginia and others are in nearby Maryland. There are easily some 270,000 federal workers in the Washington area—civilian workers. Not included are the thousands of military, naval, and air personnel in the Department of Defense, at Belvoir, Ft. Myer, Andrews Air Base, and the other installations in or about the District.

The business of the rest of the country may be business or agriculture or education or the creation and nurture of electronic computers, but the business of Washington is government.

The District's Industry

Government in all its modern-day complexities and complications is Washington's one all-embracing, overpowering, and pervasive industry. Thousands of other important and varied activities take place in Washington, but they are all peripheral. The organizations and people engaged in them are all there to serve, in one way or another, the government and the people who work for it.

They are there to feed them and house them, to entertain them, to advise them, to arm them with tools or ideas, to influence them, to sell them insurance, gasoline, trees, air conditioners, bifocals, Chihuahuas, or anything else they can persuade them to buy. Other world capitals, like London or Paris, existed long before they became seats of government and would continue to be important if the governments which

they entertain moved to better neighborhoods. Washington was created for government, exists for government, and might well disappear as a major American city if government went elsewhere.

In principle, the American federal government is simple. Deriving its powers from the Constitution, it is divided into the three familiar branches: Executive, Legislative, and Judicial. The Executive is the President, the Vice President, and their many advisers and assistants. The Legislative is the Congress, made up of the House of Representatives, the lower house, and the Senate, the upper house. The Judicial is the federal courts, with the United States Supreme Court of nine justices the most powerful in the land. This is the court of last appeal, the courts whose decisions are final.

These three branches of the federal government operate with and against each other in the well-known system of checks and balances. The democratic principle on which the government of the United States works and this triune system by which it works are as sound as

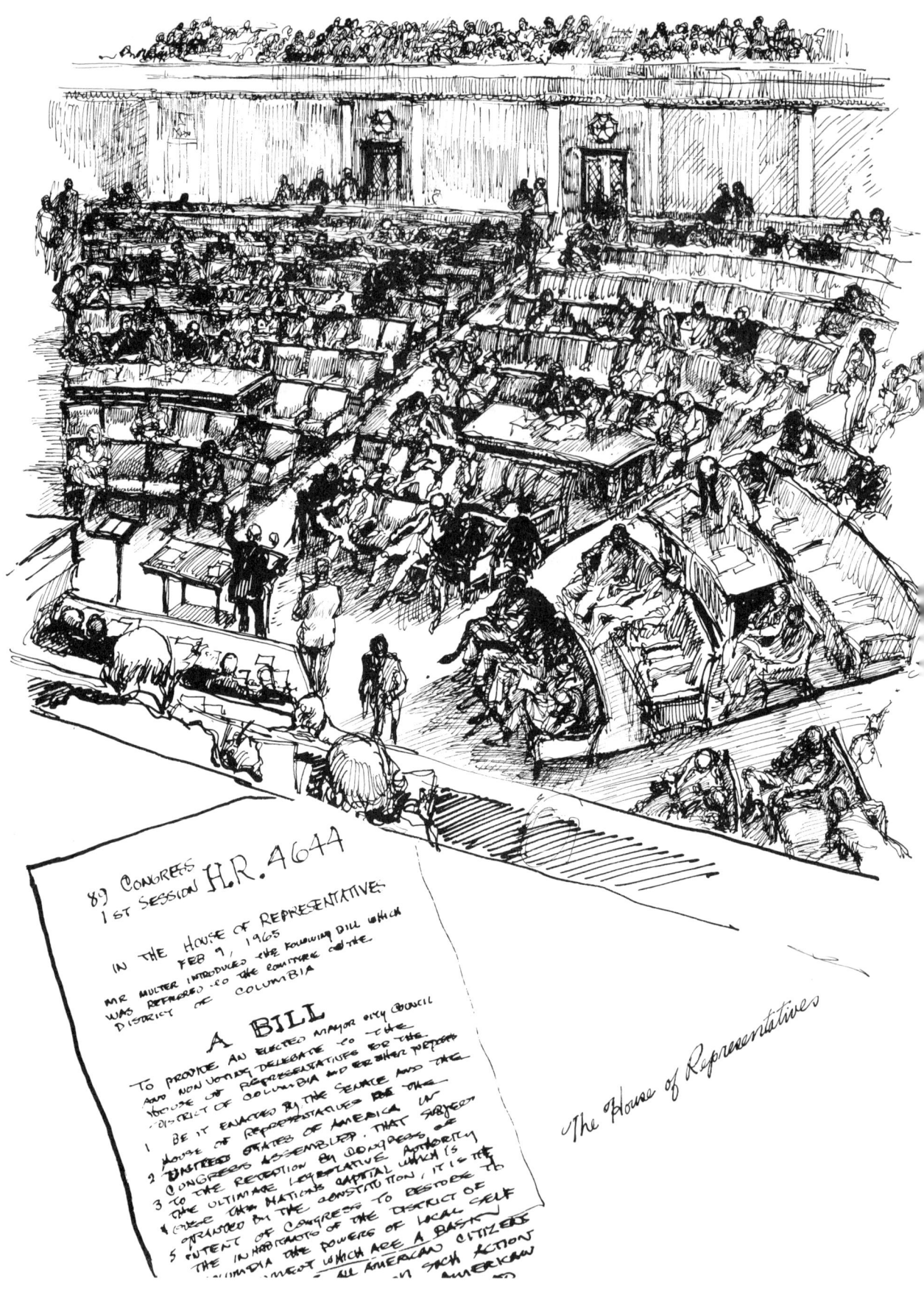

The Senate

they are simple. They are sound simply because they have proved themselves in practice.

A proposal affecting the interests of the country and the welfare of its people is made in the House. It may have been suggested originally by the President, by a party leader, by a Congressman, or by interested groups or individuals to a Congressman. When the proposal of a new law about buildings, roads, tariffs, housing, education or any of a thousand other subjects is made in the House, it becomes a bill. Usually the bill is referred to the appropriate House committee for study. The committee examines the bill, votes for or against it, and reports to the full House. The bill is discussed on the floor. If by a majority vote the House approves and passes the bill, it is sent on to the Senate for consideration.

The Senate, like the House, refers the bill to a committee which examines, discusses, debates, votes, and reports back. The bill comes to a vote in the Senate. If, again by a majority vote, the bill passes, it is then sent on to the President for his signature. When the President signs it, the bill becomes a new law of the land.

The President may not sign it. He may veto it. If he does, Congress as the duly elected representatives of the people may pass it over his head. By a vote of two-thirds in favor in both House and Senate, a bill can become law without the President's signature.

The Senate, then, checks on the judgment and actions of the House. The President checks on the judgment and actions of both the House and the Senate. Congress, in review, checks on the President's judgment and action. So operates the system of checks and balances.

There may be one more check. If there is any doubt about the constitutionality of the new law, it is referred to the Supreme Court. If the Chief Justice and his Associate Justices decide that the new law is unconstitutional, it is thrown out. It can become law then only by an amendment to the Constitution. An amendment requires the favorable vote of two-thirds of the members of both the House of Representatives and the Senate and the approval of three-fourths of all the states. This process is long and costly. Except in matters of central importance to the nation, it is seldom resorted to.

The United States Supreme Court

After a bill has become law, it is up to the Executive Branch, the branch headed by the President himself, to carry it out. This is why the Executive Branch of the federal government is by far the largest of the three. Of all the employes of the national government throughout the country, 2,461,855 work for the Executive Branch. The Army, Navy, and Air Force have large numbers of civilian workers. The Post Office alone employs nearly 590,000 workers, and there are about 175,000 in the Veterans Administration.

The Executive Branch is divided into Departments. Until 1965, when Housing and Urban Development was added, there were ten. The eleven now are: Agriculture; Commerce; Defense; Health, Education and Welfare; Interior; Justice; Labor; Post Office; State; Treasury; and Housing and Urban Development. Each of these Departments is headed by a Cabinet member: the Secretary of State, the Postmaster General, the Attorney General, and the other Secretaries.

The Departments themselves are trisected into bureaus, branches, and sections. Bureaus, like the Bureau of the Census or the National Bureau of Standards, can be very large and sections numerically very small. In the social and political hierarchy of the District of Columbia a bureau chief far outranks a branch chief who far outranks a section chief who far outranks a mere member of his section.

Big as they are, and they are very big, these 11 major government departments do not take in all the federal workers in the Executive Branch. Many are in the half a hundred independent federal agencies that range from the American Battle Monuments Commission and the Atomic Energy Commission through the Federal Trade Commission and the National Capitol Housing Authority to the Virgin Islands Corporation.

The City

Government is why Washington is, but it is only part of what it is.

Washington is a stately city of dignity and grace. It is the capital of democracy, the stronghold of the free world, and you know it when you are there. It is broad avenues and wide streets and the sense of history. George Washington was here. So were Abraham Lincoln, Theodore Roosevelt, Franklin D. Roosevelt, and John F. Kennedy. Washington is everything the United States was, is, and hopes to be, and you are conscious of that, too.

Washington is power, national and international power. It is the national mind and the nation's voice, and what that voice says is heard and heeded—Washington says . . . Washington believes . . . official Washington refuses comment . . . at his news conference this morning the President said. . . .

Washington is the flag flying in the breeze over the Capitol. A billion picture postcards and as many snapshots cannot take the thrill out of that. This is it. Here it is. Here it really is. You've seen it pictured

so many times, it is as familiar as brushing your teeth in the morning; but it is different when you are actually there. The sight touches your heart. You feel excited and proud. You can't help it. Few can.

There are as many jokes—some not jokes at all—about government inefficiency in Washington as there are about being lost in the mammoth Pentagon. There are government offices that move with the speed of a glacier. The city rings to false promises every year and echoes to the mutterings of disappointed office seekers every day. There are major and minor conspiracies. Occasionally there are full-fledged political scandals. It doesn't seem to matter. This is Washington, and it is wonderful.

Washington is being so hot you wish you could kick off your shoes and lie down on the nearest spot of shaded grass. It is standing

WASHINGTON, D.C.

in line so long to see something, you don't care whether you see it or not. If you are a government girl among thousands and thousands of government secretaries and typists, it is being so lonely sometimes you almost wish you had never heard of the place and had stayed home to do your typing in a local real estate office; only you're glad you didn't.

You're in Washington, and everyone at home envies you. You wear clothes you could not have bought at home. You live your own life in your own apartment with one, two, or a half dozen other girls to share the expense, and you know that great things are going on all about you. Just yesterday you glimpsed the President being driven down Pennsylvania Avenue or saw a turbaned diplomat, and tomorrow

The Justice Dept. Building — the F.B.I.

WASHINGTON, D.C.

you might see a famous movie star come to Washington to confer with some publicity-conscious politician. That's where the hold is. You can never go home again except for a visit. You love home, but you couldn't stand it. You've been in Washington.

Congressmen who fail to get reelected feel the same way. So do ex-Senators, ex-Cabinet members or Presidential advisers. Many manage to stay in Washington by opening law offices or becoming lobbyists. Admirals and generals and soldiers and sailors of lesser rank who have served in Washington headquarters often find it emotionally impossible to leave the District after they retire. Aged officers whose names were once familiar in the news live in the Army and Navy Club downtown. More veterans live in the United States Soldiers Home far out on North Capitol.

Washington is the FBI shooting down the cornered John Dil-

WASHINGTON, D.C.

linger, law and order triumphing over crime and evil in a stirring exhibit at the Department of Justice. It is the Bureau of Engraving turning out dollar bills and hundred dollar bills the way water pours into the kitchen sink and down the drain. It is the majesty and dignity of the Lincoln Memorial at the west end of the Mall and the Jefferson Memorial on the south shore of the Tidal Basin in West Potomac Park. It is the Washington Monument rising 555 feet $5\frac{1}{8}$ inches to make it the tallest stone and masonry structure in the world.

Washington is raising high school rumpuses in the rooms and corridors of long-suffering tourist hotels and a riotous time being had by all and wish you were here. It is standing obediently in line to look and trying politely to listen to guides and laughing more loudly than you usually do because you don't want anyone to see how deeply you are moved and don't quite understand yourself why you are.

3

Washington is the most looked at capital in the world. Over nine million people visit it every year and spend millions of dollars—it was $4,000,000 in 1964—in the city. This does not displease Washington's innkeepers, merchants, and restaurateurs. Groups, usually the senior class, which has been working and saving its money for the trip all through high school, come from some fifteen thousand schools all over the country every year.

There are times when Washington seems to be inhabited almost entirely by tourists. During the Cherry Blossom Festival in April this is just about one-third true. More than a million visitors come to Washington then, and there are about two and a half million people living in the Washington Metropolitan Area. Ask a man the way to the Smithsonian, and he is apt to say apologetically that he is from Phoenix, but perhaps the Smithsonian is that way. Ask someone else the time, and he doesn't know because he is from Los Angeles and still confused by the time difference. Let's see, is it three hours earlier or later?

Parades, balls, pageants, floats, and, of course, a queen come when the cherry blossoms are out around the Tidal Basin. Hotels and restaurants are jammed. This is spring in Washington, and it is delightful. Appearance of the blossoms on time seems to make the arrival of spring official in the United States.

Washington stages a Summer Jubilee from mid-June to early September, and the tourists pour in again by bus, train, plane, and family car. Depending on sex, the high school students who come in the spring are usually in suits or sports jackets and flannels or in dresses. It is during the summer months that the American public comes to see its capital in shorts or slacks—sex immaterial this time—and a camera.

WASHINGTON, D.C.

What all these visitors see is no longer the wilderness village of 1800 or the mud town of the Civil War period, but one of the largest cities in the United States. The population of the District itself is now about one million. The population of the Washington Metropolitan Area, which takes in Montgomery and Prince Georges counties in Maryland and Arlington, Alexandria, Fairfax, and Falls Church in Virginia, is about two and a half times that size.

Arlington Memorial Bridge
"Gateway to National Pride"

WASHINGTON, D.C.

Like other American cities, Washington (which gave back its original Virginia lands before the Civil War) has spilled over its political boundaries. Only a few years ago Bethesda, Silver Spring, and other nearby Maryland communities were discernibly separate communities and Falls Church in Virginia a village and Alexandria visibly a separate city. They have all grown to be part of the Washington urban and suburban complex, and the thickly populated suburbs have spread far beyond them all. Both downtown Washington and the suburbs are still growing rapidly. Billions of dollars are being spent in the District for new public and private buildings.

The master plan of the National Capital Planning Commission is based on an estimate of a Washington area population of five million by the year 2000. This Commission and the Commission on Fine Arts are both behind the plan to redesign Pennsylvania Avenue so that it will be the grand boulevard from the White House to the Capitol that L'Enfant envisioned. Another plan is to make the Mall from Capitol Hill to the Lincoln Memorial a promenade of little parks with fountains, bookstalls, and outdoor eating places after the European manner. New hotels have been built in Washington; old ones torn down. Foggy Bottom, an old section in a bend of the Potomac above Constitution Avenue, is being so rebuilt and refurbished that the name it earned from the presence of a brewery and a huge gas works will hardly seem fitting any more.

Much of this the visitor can see going on about him if he cares to look. Why should he? He can see the same kinds of things going on at home. What he has come to see is something else.

He has come to see the marble and granite, the glass and steel and concrete, the embodiment of an ideal. He has come to see where Abraham Lincoln walked and talked. He wants to see where Calhoun and Webster and Clay and all the others were before him. He wants to feel the greatness of the past and for a little while be near the men who are shaping his country's present and its future. He wants to see the documents of American freedom, to shake hands with a Congressman or a Senator, to look at the row of classic government buildings—Com-

WASHINGTON, D.C.

merce, Labor, the Post Office, Justice—which face on Constitution and back on Pennsylvania in the Federal Triangle, and to see a Supreme Court Justice or watch the pacing of one of the honor guards at the Tomb of the Unknown Soldier. If he is lucky, he will see the beautiful Pan-American Union, with its Aztec Gardens, its Hall of Heroes, and its Hall of the Americas, at 17th and Constitution Avenue. One thing he will certainly see. It is the tallest thing in sight.

The Washington Monument

The Washington Monument, on the Mall between 15th and 16th Streets, N.W., dominates the Washington skyline, just as during his lifetime George Washington dominated the uncertain new country he had fathered. The severe marble shaft tapering high into the sky says George Washington and says Washington, District of Columbia, to all the world. Beautiful in its soaring simplicity, the Washington Monument seems to have grown where it stands, but it did not get there easily.

WASHINGTON, D.C.

L'Enfant had picked the exact spot for a memorial to George Washington. The ground proved too marshy. Another site was chosen nearby, and in 1833, the Washington Monument Society began trying to collect $1,000,000 to raise a monument. Fourteen years later, only $87,000 had been collected by hard door-to-door selling, but work was begun in 1847 to raise the shaft designed by Robert Mills. At Fourth of July ceremonies at the site in 1850, President Taylor sat in the sun eating a bag of cherries and washing them down with cold milk. He died during the week.

Inscribed memorial stones to be built into the monument, which has walls 15 feet thick at the bottom, but only 18 inches thick at the top, came from various nations abroad, from Indian tribes, and from patriotic societies. In 1854, Pope Pius IX sent a block of African marble marked, "Rome to America." During the night it was stolen and smashed to pieces. Work on the monument stopped for 22 years. A truncated shaft 150 feet tall stood abandoned in Washington until building was resumed in 1876 when Congress appropriated the money needed to complete the $1,187,710 project.

When the Washington Monument was finally completed in 1884, the newspapers proudly reported that the obelisk was the tallest structure on earth. It was 43 feet higher than the Cologne Cathedral. If the Sphinx were placed on top of St. Paul's in London, it would still fall 100 feet short of the country's lasting tribute to its founder. The Washington Monument was opened to the public October 9, 1888, and the public has thronged it ever since. Whenever it is open, which is some part of every day except Christmas, there are large crowds waiting to ascend to the top in the elevator or to climb the 898 steps past the 190 memorial stones to see the superb view of Washington and Virginia afforded from the peak.

Lincoln Memorial

If the American past can be identified with two names, the names are George Washington and Abraham Lincoln, one the father and the other the savior of his country. Together they merge into what, in

current parlance, is the image of the United States in the emotions of its people. Thus it is fitting that the other great memorial in Washington is to Lincoln. Both monuments are splendid. Both typify, but there is a difference. The Washington Monument is one of the sights of the capital and a height from which other sights can be seen. The Lincoln Memorial is more nearly a shrine.

Uncle Joe Cannon, for many years dictatorial Speaker of the House, was derisive when in 1911 the Fine Arts Commission proposed to erect a Greek temple housing a 21-foot tall seated figure of Lincoln in Potomac Park. It was then Potomac Flats and a bog. Any memorial placed there, said Uncle Joe, would shake itself down with loneliness and ague.

After President William Howard Taft turned the first spadeful of earth, it took an entire year to build the foundation by sinking over one hundred giant steel cylinders into the ground until they reached solid rock, filling these with solid concrete, then building a base on this support. On it was erected the temple facing the Reflecting Pool (it was called The Lagoon then), the Washington Monument, and the dome of the Capitol on "the Hill."

The 36 Doric columns of the outside of the temple represent the 36 states that were in the Union at the time of Lincoln's assassination. Inside, Ionic columns separate the north and south chambers from the central chamber in which Lincoln, in the statue that took Daniel Chester French four years to carve from 28 blocks of white marble, gazes out over the country he preserved. The familiar but always moving words of Lincoln's Second Inaugural and of his Gettysburg Address are inscribed in the Memorial. The Lincoln Memorial is beautifully proportioned. It reflects the dignity, simplicity, even the homeliness of Abraham Lincoln. The Washington Monument awes through its spearlike height and towering dominance. The Lincoln Memorial compels reverence.

Washington is a city of monuments and memorials. One, fortunately, is inimitable. This is the heroic equestrian statue of President Andrew Jackson in Lafayette Park across Pennsylvania Avenue from the White House. For reasons made obvious by a glance, it is known as

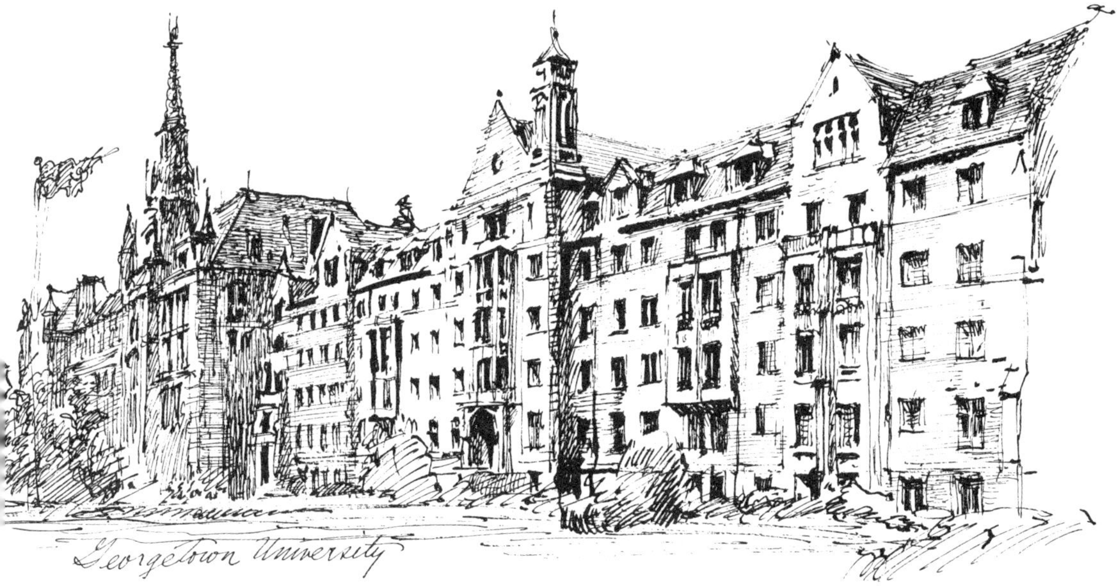
Georgetown University

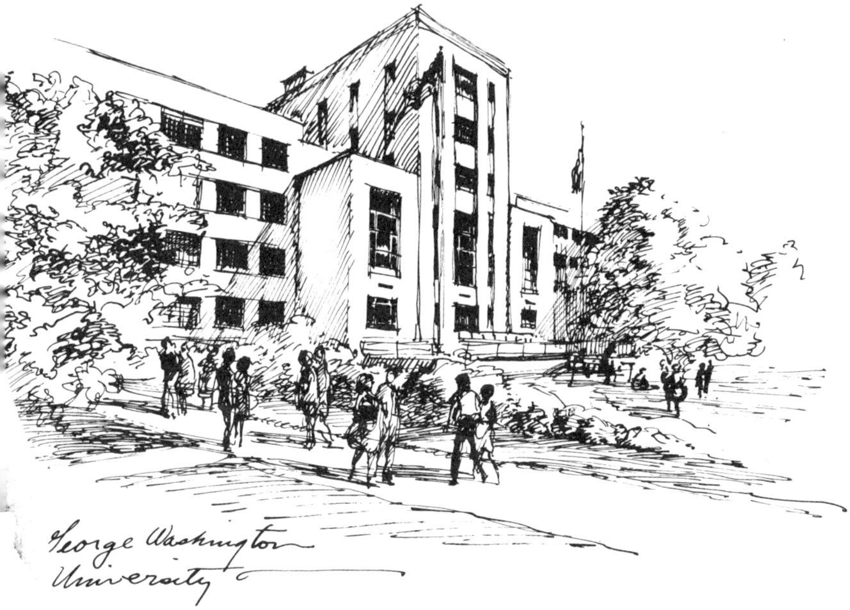
George Washington
University

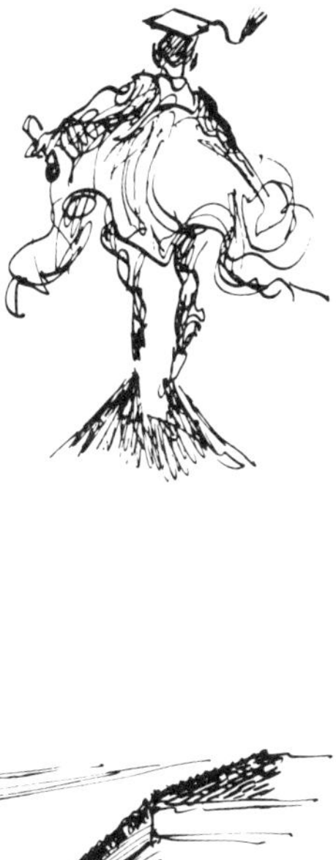

Catholic University

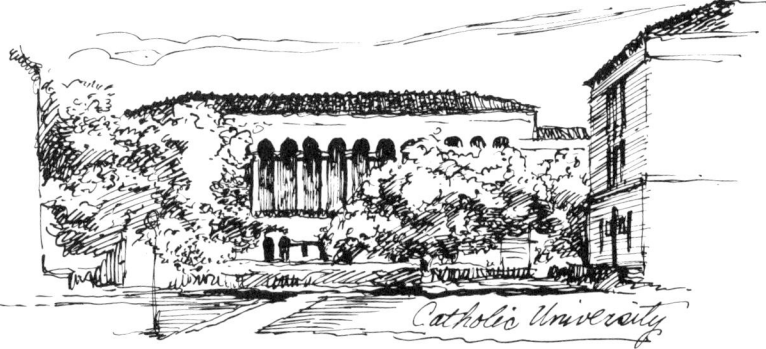

WASHINGTON, D.C.

the "hobby horse" statue. It made Lincoln laugh every time he saw it. Lincoln was living at this time in 1600 Pennsylvania Avenue, the White House.

The White House

Though Theodore Roosevelt was the first to make that its official name, L'Enfant's "President's Palace" actually became the White House when its walls were painted white to hide the smoke-blackened stone after the British had burned it in 1814. The home of every American President since John Adams, the White House may well be the most beautiful structure in Washington. Perhaps because it is lived in and is alive with memories of the men, women, children, and pets who have lived in it since 1800, because the great of the earth have dined and danced and talked and slept there, because the bright and brilliant

men and women of the country have been honored there, the White House seems the living heart of Washington and of the country.

The Capitol is talk and noise. It has echoed to resounding rhetoric and even the cries of physical violence. Emotions enough have been felt there; but the Capitol is a cold place, a place of business, the country's business. The White House is the country's home. It is the warmth and color of Dolly Madison, the girth of Grover Cleveland, the lank humor of Lincoln, the Theodore Roosevelt children at play, Fala at the feet of Franklin D. Roosevelt in his wheel chair. It is Caroline Kennedy and her pony, Macaroni, President Eisenhower putting golf balls on the lawn, President Truman striding out for his early morning walk. Limousines slip noiselessly up the curving drives to Presidential receptions. The building was brilliantly lighted for the many parties during the Kennedy administration. It is the center of Washington social life.

The White House is stately and imposing. It is also warm and unpretentious. There have been births, marriages, and deaths in the White House as in most American homes. There have been young brides like Frances Folsom, who was married in the East Room to Grover Cleveland, and failing statesmen like Woodrow Wilson. The past and the living present seem to merge in the White House, and the blood of the nation seems to course through it. It is continually in the news. Everyone knows what it looks like, but it never seems to stale. This may be in part because of its proportions and its setting. The fastidious Henry James called it "the graceful thing in Washington beyond any other."

Hoban designed it, Halleck built it, Latrobe helped rebuild it. Jefferson planned the grounds and planted the rows of poplars down Pennsylvania Avenue. Andrew Jackson had the main entrance face Pennsylvania and the north instead of south to the Potomac. Gas light was installed under Van Buren, central heating under Fillmore. Buchanan added a greenhouse. Theodore Roosevelt added the office wings. Badly weakened over the years, the entire White House was structurally strengthened during the Truman administration and done over at a cost of nearly six million dollars. Mrs. John F. Kennedy redecorated much of the interior.

WASHINGTON, D.C.

Twice each morning except Sundays, Mondays, and holidays, long lines of people queue up outside the East Wing opposite the Treasury to see the public rooms of the White House under the guidance of the black-uniformed White House Police. Officers of this picked force of 200 men stand quietly along the line of march, and one of their number acts as guide. The first group admitted are those who have procured invitations from Congressmen or other dignitaries; the second, who begin their slow passage through at ten o'clock in the morning, are the general public.

WASHINGTON, D.C.

These visitors see the oval Diplomatic Reception Room on the ground floor, the Grand Foyer on the main floor, then, in succession, the State Dining Room, the Red Room, the Blue Room, the Green Room, and the East Room. The total impression is of spaciousness and richness yet dignity and restraint. The silken hangings, the oil portraits, the silver and gilt, the china, the antique furniture blend for a pervasive effect of elegance, subdued grandeur, and charm.

As he enters through the lower hall the visitor passes busts of Presidents, glimpses the wide south lawns and gardens. He may even catch sight of a member of the President's family going to or from the hidden elevator that leads to the "President's House" on the second and third floors. The President himself may hurry past with a wave and a smile on his way to some appointment in the West Wing.

The President's House is the private home of the President and his family. Only invited guests may ascend to the 54-room mansion with its 16 baths and its private kitchens. In it are the Lincoln Bedroom and the Rose Guest Room, known, too, as the Queen's Bedroom, for five queens have slept there.

The White House is almost a self-sustaining community. Out of sight underground, some below the lawns, are the steward's office, a room for flower arranging, a carpentry shop, an electric nerve center, a paint shop, an upholstery shop, and storage vaults behind blast-proof steel doors. In the East Wing are the squad rooms of the White House Police, the office of the President's military aide, and a room in which engraved invitations to formal White House functions are lettered in matching calligraphy.

WASHINGTON, D.C.

The more important West Wing houses the office of the President, the Cabinet meeting room, the offices of the Presidential aides and assistants. On the lowest level of the wing are the Navy-staffed dispensary, a sound communications center, and a Navy mess for the use of top White House aides and their guests. In this wing also is one of the most closely guarded rooms in Washington, the Situation Room. Twenty-four hours a day, news from all sources, often top secret, is channeled into it to keep the President quickly and fully informed on every subject affecting national security.

When he revisited the United States in 1825, Lafayette kept a pet alligator in the great East Room for a time. Tad and Willie Lincoln raced their team of goats there, and later, Garfield's sons used it as a bicycle track when bicycles were new. Once when a Prince of Wales brought too large a retinue with him, President Buchanan had to sleep in the hall. During World War I, President Wilson kept a herd of sheep on the lawn. When their wool was auctioned off, it brought $100,000, which the President gave to the Red Cross. The White House has a past. It has a present. While the visitor is gazing at a crystal chandelier or at the Presidential Seal in the Grand Foyer, a secret meeting of the President and his advisers may be taking place not far from where he is standing, or some momentous decision may be being reached.

The Capitol

The Capitol of the United States is vast. It is imposing, intricately ornate, thronged, and again vast. It is a huge pile of stone and masonry, statuary, heroic murals, oil paintings, and it is busy or curious people.

Almost a city in itself, the Capitol was meant to be vast and impressive. It was built to impress the rest of the world with the sovereignty of the United States and the grandeur of its future. These were dreams and ambitions in 1800. They are realities now, and the domed, floodlighted Capitol says that they are. Massive and immovable, the Capitol stands as the chief architectural symbol of an established world power.

Senate Wing

Statue of 'Freedom' atop Capitol Dome.

Essentially, the Capitol is one central building with two huge wings. The rotunda in the center is 97 feet across and rises 180 feet to the great Capitol dome. The wing to the north houses the Senate Chamber, that to the south the chamber of the House of Representatives. The ground plan is simple, but the Capitol has long been a huge complex of offices, committee rooms, restaurants, a post office, a barber shop, an empty crypt where George Washington was to have been entombed, a subway, and all the other appurtenances necessary to a place of business in which 100 Senators and nearly 450 Representatives pass thousands of bills a year and appropriate billions on billions of dollars to run the mammoth federal government.

WASHINGTON, D.C.

As familiar a sign of American freedom as the Liberty Bell in Philadelphia or the Statue of Liberty in New York harbor, the Capitol is redolent of the whole American past. Every statesman who has been part of American history and American thought has spoken here. Presidents have addressed combined sessions of the Senate and the House at times of great crisis. Heroes returning from celebrated victories—as General Eisenhower after his return from liberated Europe in World War II and General MacArthur after his recall from the Orient—have spoken memorable words in this place.

For fifty years the House met in what is now the statuary room, crowded with the stone-carved likenesses of public men of the various states. It was here that Abraham Lincoln sat when he was a Congressman. John Quincy Adams, who served in the House for 17 years after he had been President, fell from his desk here in February 1848 and died.

In what was the Senate Chamber from 1819 to 1859, Vice President Aaron Burr (only the vote of the House in 1802 had made Jefferson instead of him President when each received the same number of electoral votes) presided at the impeachment trial of Chief Justice Samuel Chase. This was in 1805. Chase was acquitted. Two years later, Burr himself was tried for treason by Chief Justice John Marshall. He also was acquitted. Daniel Webster, Henry Clay, Stephen A. Douglas, and John C. Calhoun, all held forth in this room. Here Congressman Preston S. Brooks of South Carolina attacked and nearly killed Charles Sumner, Abolitionist Senator from Massachusetts, while Sumner sat at his desk. The Capitol knew scenes of violence and of sadness just before the Civil War. Senator Jefferson Davis of Mississippi bade his colleagues farewell when he retired upon secession of his state and went home to become President of the Confederacy.

In the rotunda, under the great dome, the bodies of Presidents have lain in state: Lincoln, Grant, Garfield, McKinley, Harding, Taft, Franklin D. Roosevelt, and John F. Kennedy. Every four years a newly elected or re-elected President makes the ceremonial journey from the White House to take the oath of office on the Capitol steps, then retraces the route in a spectacle that is partly a triumphal parade, partly a political celebration; partly ceremony and partly circus.

WASHINGTON, D.C.

These are the things that the visitors who stream through the Capitol every day under the leadership of well-informed guides come to hear about and to feel. They come to see the place they have heard about all their lives, to share in the pride of ownership, and, if they can, to see Congress in action. As earlier visitors used to be disturbed by the tobacco-chewing and spittoons, the snuff-taking, the loud talk, and the papers littering the floor, those who get into the visitors' gallery of the House today are often a little shocked to see the empty seats, the legislators reading newspapers or gossiping, the general air of careless inattention.

That appearance is deceptive. Many members may be busy in important committee meetings. Others are conferring with political leaders, even with the President perhaps. Some are in conference with the constituents they represent and whose votes keep them in office. All know when their presence on the floor and their votes are needed to pass some measure favored by their party. The business of the country is not being neglected. It is going forward in the House and in the somewhat more dignified Senate Chamber every waking hour of every day when Congress is in session. The real work is being done out of sight. As in any other business, it is in the plant, not in the front office that the product or service is being hammered out. The Congressmen are as anxious as the country to get that business done, for not until the work of the session, which begins the first Monday in January, has been concluded, usually late in the summer, can they return home to campaign.

The White House and the Capitol are the central figures in the mosaic which is Washington, but many other brightly colored stones piece out the wonderful composite: the white marble Supreme Court; the Archives, where the Declaration of Independence, the Constitution, and the Bill of Rights, handwritten originals on over-sized parchments, are enshrined; the Library of Congress, where there are more than forty-one million books and where every original piece of printing —even designs on cloth—can be copyrighted; the Smithsonian Institution, founded by an Englishman, which houses some fifty-five million exhibits. If you want to see it, whatever *it* is, it is probably in the Smithsonian somewhere if you can find it.

WASHINGTON, D.C.

You can't see everything in Washington, not on one visit or a half dozen, perhaps not in a lifetime. The wise go where they most wish to be and to see. Next to the Smithsonian, at 6th and Constitution Avenue, N.W., is the National Gallery of Art. Often called the Mellon Gallery, it was given to the people of the United States by Andrew W. Mellon, wealthy Secretary of the Treasury from 1921 to 1932.

The National Gallery is one of the world's richest and most magnificent. It has gardens, concerts, a cafeteria, but the greatness of the white marble gallery is its matchless possessions, the best work of master artists of the past in many countries. It is a treasury of sculpture and painting. Raphael, Fra Angelico, Donatello, Botticelli, and Rembrandt are here. So are Sir Joshua Reynolds, Constable, Cézanne, and Americans like James Whistler and Winslow Homer. You can revel in art of the Italian Renaissance, in Oriental art, in the French impressionists, or in what you will at the National Gallery, or if you have other tastes and cherish nature as well as art, you can go a little farther out.

The National Arboretum at 28th and M Streets, N.E., has hillsides of flowering shrubs and plants. Scent mingles with sight in the beauty here. Walk the gracious Holly Trail through stands and plantings of American and English and Chinese and Japanese hollies. You can enjoy a world-famous painting in Washington or the glossy green leaves and bright fruit of a tree that was a favorite with George Washington. He would not have chopped down a holly. He planted hollies instead.

National Cathedral

All the great monuments and institutions in Washington are not governmental. Begun in 1893 when Congress granted the charter that created the Protestant Episcopal Cathedral Foundation, the Washington Cathedral—its real name is the Cathedral Church of St. Peter and St. Paul—towers up from Wisconsin Avenue and Woodley Road, miles from downtown Washington. When the Gothic structure has been completed, it will be the sixth largest church in the world. This awe-inspiring church houses ecclesiastical richness of all the kinds expected of the great cathedrals of the world: the soaring architecture,

National Shrine of the Immaculate Conception

within the Mosque

Islamic Center

the carvings in stone and wood, the silken banners of the church. Around the great nave and transept are the beautiful chapels: the Children's Chapel, St. John's Chapel, St. Mary's Chapel, and the others. The glorious Bethlehem Chapel in the ambulatory with its beautiful stained glass windows was the first part of the Cathedral to be completed. Services have been held in it since 1912. The tomb of President Wilson is in the Cathedral, and memorials to other American statesmen are there.

On the 57-acre close of the Cathedral grounds are the National Cathedral School for Girls, the St. Alban's School for Boys, an elementary school, and conference centers for clergymen and for church musicians. The Bishop's Garden with its famed old English boxwood is a delightful place. Near it is a small herb garden, and not far away, a gilded equestrian statue of George Washington dominates a landscaped slope. Whether seen from the outside or viewed from the inside where the light pours down through great rose windows in cascading colors, the National Cathedral compels awe and reverence. The Cathedral is the seat of two bishops, the Presiding Bishop of the Episcopal Church in the United States and the Bishop of the Diocese of Washington.

WASHINGTON, D.C.

In the recently opened Manuscript Room there is a Gutenberg Bible, 1455, beautifully bound in gold-tooled red morocco. There is also a copy of the first Rheims-Douay Bible printed in the United States; it was issued in Philadelphia by Matthew Carey in 1790.

Folger Library

Another world-renowned book is housed in the Folger Library on East Capitol Street near the Supreme Court. The Folger has not just one copy but many of the famous 1623 folio of the plays of William Shakespeare. It has copies of every work by and about Shakespeare that can be found, for this is the Shakespeare library of the world. The library itself is for the use of scholars, but it contains displays which will fascinate the layman. The interior of the stone building is largely Elizabethan, and the Exhibition Hall contains both a reproduction of a great hall of the period and a small-scale Globe Playhouse, the kind of theater in which Shakespeare's plays were originally produced.

National Geographic

Alexander Graham Bell, inventor of the telegraph, was a well-known and greatly honored Washington resident. A tall, portly man of gentle manner, he lived in a $100,000 mansion near Scott Circle. Among other things, he was president of the National Geographic Society, which was founded in 1888 at a meeting of Washington's famed Cosmos Club. In 1899, Bell appointed his 23-year-old son-in-law, Gilbert Grosvenor, editor of the Society's *National Geographic Magazine*. Sole employe of the Society, Grosvenor carried the entire 1,000 copies of the first issue he edited to the post office himself. Grosvenor edited the magazine for 55 years, and when the Society celebrated its seventy-fifth anniversary in 1963, the magazine's circulation was more than 3,500,000.

The *National Geographic* is so famous for the explorations it has sponsored or supported and for its reports and maps that many people assume it is an agency of the U.S. government. Early in 1964, the

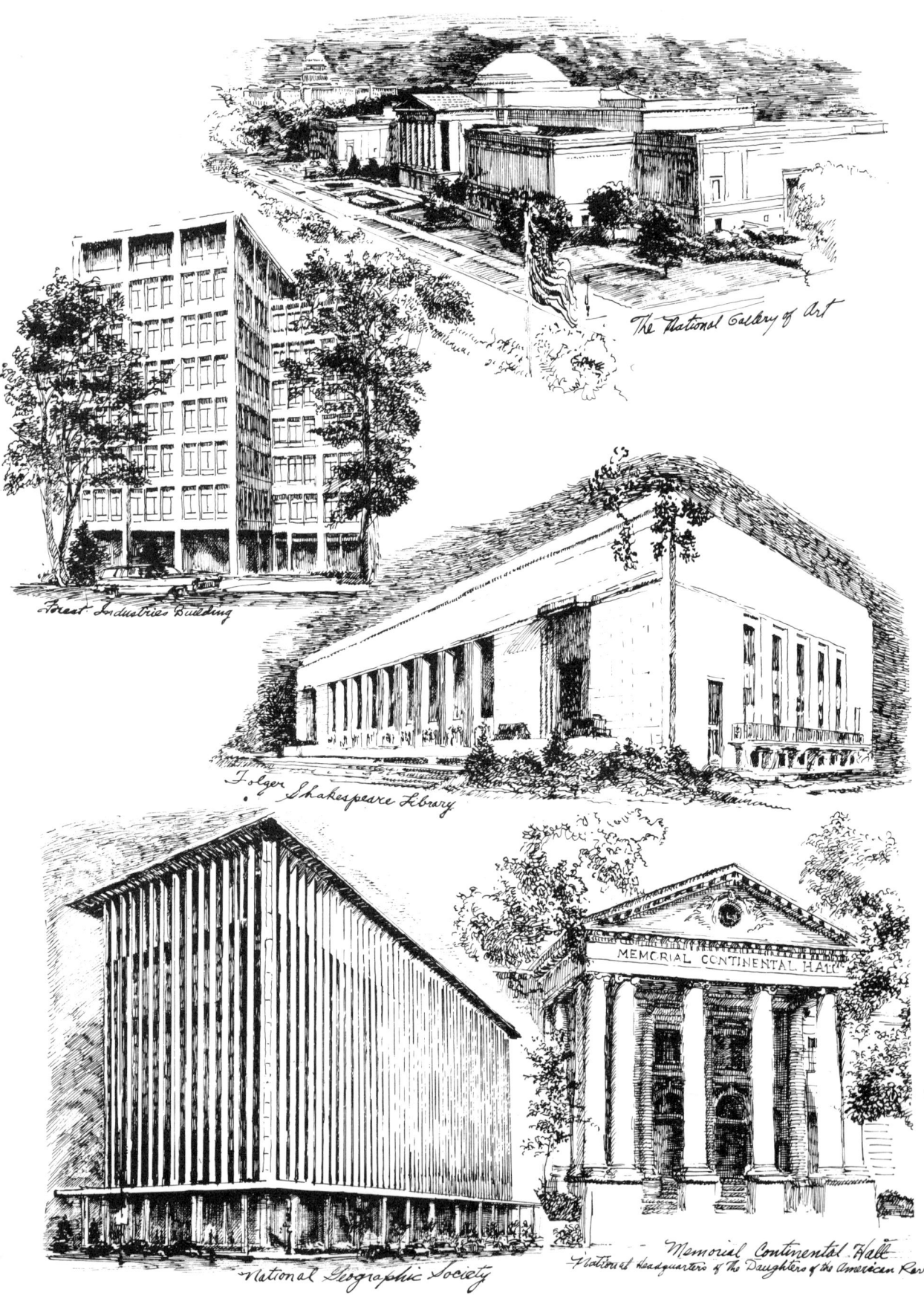

WASHINGTON, D.C.

Society, long established on 16th Street, moved into a striking new building at 17th and M. The Explorers Hall on the main floor with its huge, slowly rotating globe of the world and its exhibits of Arctic, Antarctic, and space exploration provides a colorful and very modern audio-visual experience.

Arlington National Cemetery

One Washington memorial belongs in spirit neither to government nor to private enterprise. It belongs to the dead of the country's wars. Across the Potomac on the rolling Virginia countryside, Arlington National Cemetery was founded in 1864 about the home of General Robert E. Lee. Some 126,000 servicemen or members of their families, the known, the little known, and the unknown, are buried there.

President William Howard Taft is buried in Arlington. So are John Foster Dulles, William Jennings Bryan, Robert Todd Lincoln,

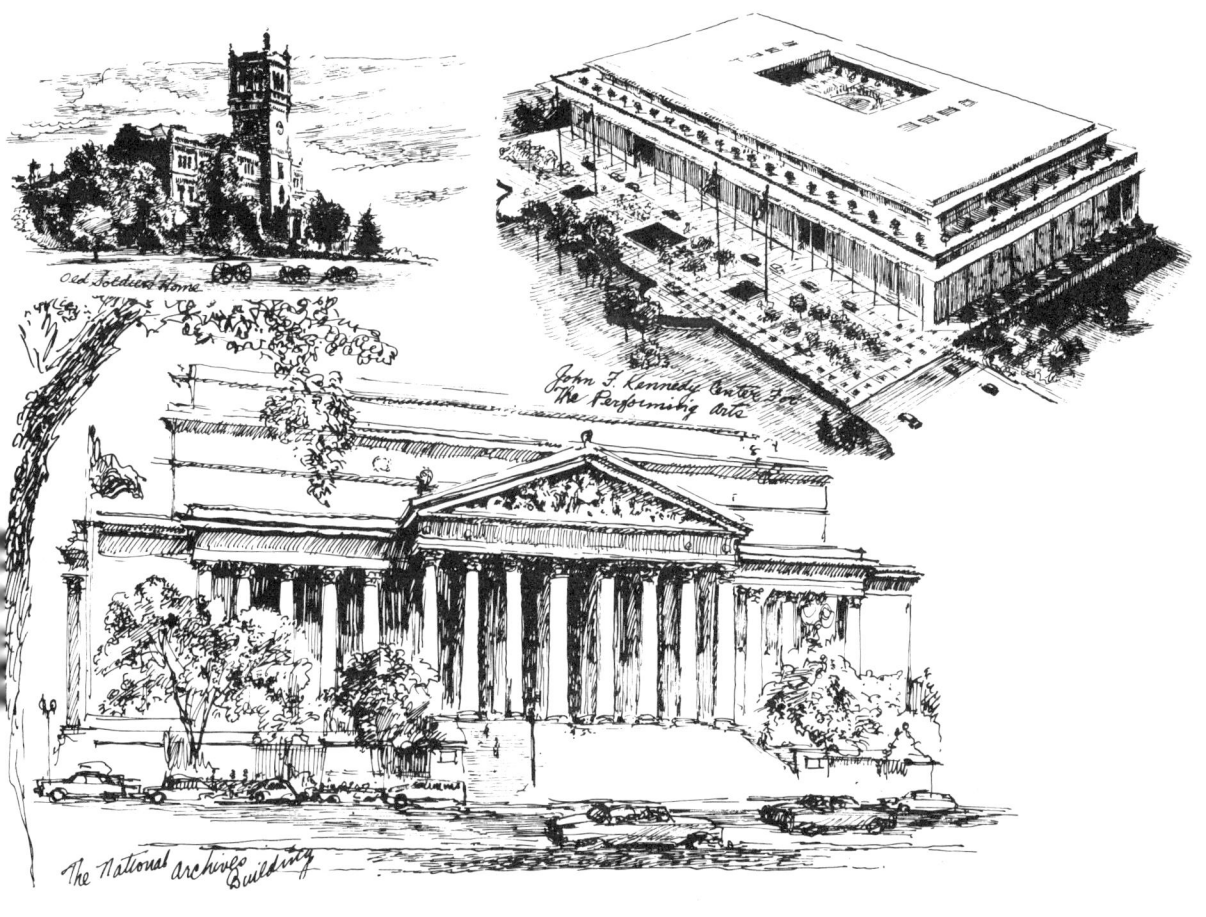

WASHINGTON, D.C.

John J. Pershing, L'Enfant, Jonathan Wainwright, Robert E. Perry, Richard E. Byrd, and President John F. Kennedy. Soldiers of Washington's army lie there. So do 2,000 men who died at Bull Run and 229 men who were killed when the U.S. Battleship "Maine" exploded in Havana harbor in 1898.

Every hour on the hour the honor guard is changed before the Tomb of the Unknown Soldier. Originally this was the resting place of a nameless victim of World War I. It is now in addition the grave of an unknown casualty of World War II and of the Korean War.

4

Washington, d.c., owes its location to a political deal between Thomas Jefferson and Alexander Hamilton. It owes its existence as a modern city to a political boss, Boss Shepherd.

Alexander Robey Shepherd, a giant of a man, was a very successful plumber who became an alderman, a newspaper owner, president of the City Reform Association and, when the District was made a territory of the United States in 1871, first its vice president and then its president.

Overriding all opposition, he began to transform a squalid town into a shining metropolis. Hiring anybody and everybody in any fashion he chose—it was during Grant's administration, which was not noted for scrupulousness—he awarded contracts where he willed and to whom he wished. L'Enfant had had the dream. Shepherd went recklessly about making it a reality. He turned loose armies of workmen to pave miles of Washington's streets, put in sidewalks, install adequate water and sewage systems, create parks, and plant fast-growing trees. He exceeded his authority and ignored budgets, protests, and difficulties alike. Boss Shepherd very nearly bankrupted the city—Congress had to appropriate money to save it—but he got the job done.

A Congressional investigation of his questionable methods brought an end to his reign and an end to the three years of territorial government. Virtually expelled from Washington, Shepherd went to Mexico, vowing he would not return until he had enough money to buy the city. He did not make that much, but when he returned to Washington in 1887, he was greeted, as he deserved to be, as a conquering hero.

WASHINGTON, D.C.

In appearance, today's Washington dates really from Boss Shepherd and the 1870s as much as from L'Enfant and the 1790s. It is a city of broad avenues and wide, tree-shaded streets, a city of green parks and open spaces. There are patches of lawn, shrubs, and flowers everywhere, hundreds of them. Both government and private buildings are kept low by law. Washington is an open city. You are never hemmed in. Life feels different from what it does in lower or midtown Manhattan or in Chicago's Loop.

Little parks and big parks characterize Washington. Potomac Park of some 740 acres in the southeast part of the District extends into the spacious mile-long Mall. Rock Creek Park, a beautiful expanse of unspoiled woodland, fields, roads, and byways, runs for many miles from a point on the Potomac about opposite Theodore Roosevelt Island north into Maryland. Only a few minutes from downtown, you are truly in the country in Rock Creek, where you may have to ford streams that in several places run across the shaded roads, and where, with a little inattention, you can easily get lost.

As late as the 1890s, Washington was and was called a city of boarding houses. Its political population then, as now, was transient. Congressmen and clerks lived in apartments and hotels. Washington still has a large transient population made up of officeholders, military and naval personnel on tours of duty or special assignment, experts called in for brief periods, businessmen come to plead their causes or sell their wares. Many people live in furnished quarters and eat their meals in restaurants.

Yet Washington long since has also been and has been called a city of homes. The city's permanent population of Civil Service workers and of business and professional people are its real population. Proverbially, its noncommissioned officers run the Army and its chiefs the Navy. The career Civil Service men and women who stay on administration after administration run the federal government departments and agencies and accomplish their day-to-day routine work. The doctors, lawyers, dry cleaners, dentists, and grocers stay on just as they stay on in any other community where people eat, wear clothes, get sore throats, and have the toothache. The celebrities come and go, but the real people of Washington remain. Most of these live in their own homes, almost always well and proudly cared for, in the residential sections of the city and in suburban Virginia and Maryland. These areas abound in greenery, in lawns, shrubs, gardens.

Horticulturally, Washington is southern. Redbud and crepe myrtle, camellias, dogwood, and holly make Washington look more like Charleston or Atlanta than like gray Philadelphia, brisk New York, or frozen Boston. There are luxuriant plantings around hotels, homes, and office buildings, just as there are in government domains. Much of the pleasantness of Washington comes from its green and leafy look, abundant nature skillfully nurtured and landscaped by man. Washington vistas are soothing. The setting for national and international statesmanship and for political disputes is almost idyllic.

Life in Washington can seem idyllic. There is no manufacturing industry of any size. There is no large-scale commerce or finance. It is in essence a genteel city. A white-haired little woman with bright eyes explained it to me one day as we waited together on K Street for a bus. "Washington is a Sunday city," she said happily. "You can wear your good clothes all the time."

You can. You may come to grief in them, for Washington's violent crime rate is high, but the city is the kind of place that makes you want to wear your best. It seems to deserve it.

People react to their surroundings. A man or a woman may be doing much the same thing that thousands of others are doing in other offices in Cleveland or Houston, but he is doing it in Washington.

WASHINGTON, D.C.

Even if you are only punching holes in cards or separating the green from the pink slips, it seems to be more important than doing the same thing on the thirty-fourth or the fifty-sixth floor of a New York skyscraper or in an ultra-modern air-conditioned one-story plant in, say, Marietta, Georgia. In other places you can't touch elbows with a statue of Lafayette or Grant on the way to work or walk through little parks between beds of tulips or glimpse the White House or the Capitol dome through the window of your bus.

No matter how unimportant—or important, for that matter—your job, it has something to do with matters of national or international significance, or it might have, or it is near such affairs of import. There is a satisfaction in this awareness. A soldier on duty at the Tomb of the Unknown Soldier feels it. So does a Congressman, a Cabinet member, a White House Policeman, an officer stationed in the Pentagon, a worker in the Department of Agriculture. The gas station attendant filling the tank of a salesman, an admiral, or a keeper in the National Zoological Park feels it, too. There is something in the air of Washington besides humidity. People are glad to be there, as they are not necessarily glad to be somewhere else.

Except on the highest echelons where crisis is commonplace, life in Washington is leisurely. The pace is slow. There is none of the energy of New York or Detroit. There is no particular hurry. Government has a monopoly of governing. It is not in competition with anybody. It does not have to be. It is not dependent on its own efforts for support. Government does not earn; it spends, and, in theory at any rate, its income is inexhaustible. Through heavy corporate taxation and heavy taxes on individual incomes, it comes from the energies of all of the country's employed citizenry. As long as that energy lasts and is productive, government income is secure. When this source fails to suffice, the government can always borrow through the sale of bonds. Its credit is good.

Because of this, Washington is a prosperous city. It does not suffer in the usual way from economic depressions. When the business of the rest of the country is good, Washington's is good. When the business of the rest of the country is bad, Washington's is still good and usually

WASHINGTON, D.C.

improves as measures are taken to alleviate the national condition. Civil Service salaries are good to high. Jobs are secure, promotions reasonably assured; vacation and sick leave provisions are very liberal, and pensions are certain. Ranking officials of the government are well paid, and officers assigned to the various military installations in and about Washington are usually of fairly high rank, with consequent high pay and allowances. The embassies and legations and the myriads of lobbying organizations spend freely. Exclusive of the military, the annual federal government payroll in the Washington area is about $1,250,000,000. Federal construction money comes to about another $7,000,000 a year. District government and the governments of the suburban areas add substantially to these sums, and tourism brings in its millions of dollars more each year.

Another business pervades the District of Columbia and adds substantially to the city's activity and income. Washington bulges with lobbyists and associations, men and women who are there to watch out for the interests of their employers. They are there to give the government the facts regarding their industries or organizations, to get and report back facts of interest to their principals or their membership, and, if they can, to persuade Congressmen, Senators, and other government officials to the points of view they represent.

There must be well over twelve hundred organizations of one kind and another—associations, councils, brotherhoods, institutes, societies —which have their national headquarters or important offices in Washington. Name almost any profession, political, business, labor, social, or political group, and there is an organization in Washington to work for it. Nursing, bottlers, textiles, pipe welding, bedding manufacturers, sleeping car porters, reserve officers, wire reinforcement, doctors, lawyers, material handling, meat packers, retail clerks, government employes, scrap metal, editors, psychiatrists, audio-visual, bituminous concrete: they are all in the list, which stretches from here to considerably beyond there.

Washington has associations for the promulgation or the prevention or the obliteration of many, many things. The AFL-CIO has its building on northwest 16th Street; the National Education Association

WASHINGTON, D.C.

is only a block away. The splendid building of the International Brotherhood of Teamsters is near the Capitol; the American Institute of Architects has the Octagon House, the Georgian mansion on New York Avenue in which James and Dolly Madison lived after the destruction of the White House during the War of 1812.

All of Washington associations are not as splendidly housed, though many have attractive buildings of their own. The oldest national forest conservation organization in the country, The American Forestry Association has a small, pleasantly proportioned building on northwest 17th Street. Fittingly, a crosscut disc of giant redwood rests on its lawn. Some of the other associations in Washington have splendid suites in office buildings, work in converted mansions, have offices in the big National Press Club building, or manage somehow in offices scattered about the federal city.

Washington does well. The big department stores like Woodward & Lothrop on F Street—"Woody's" in Washington—are usually crowded, as are their suburban branches. There are many specialty shops, fine antique shops in Georgetown and Alexandria as well as downtown in the District itself. Washington is not a discount-house town. Typically, prices are high for the high-quality and often luxury merchandise that Washington's high-income, well-educated families demand. The catering business, of course, is always good because there are so many parties.

WASHINGTON, D.C.

At the inaugural of President James Buchanan, March 4, 1857, there was food and drink at the White House: 400 gallons of oysters, 500 quarts of chicken salad, 60 saddles of mutton, 4 of venison. There were 75 hams, 125 tongues, 1,200 gallons of ice cream, and $3,000 worth of wines. The victors are hungry and thirsty after an election, and they stay that way.

Washington has always been a party town. It has the time, the money, the personable society at whatever level, and the excuse. There are always new people, people coming and going, important people, celebrated people, or just lonely people. There are parties in the White House, in the glittering embassies, in mansions and suburban homes, in costly hotels, and in much humbler and less impressive apartments. Party-giving and party-going are as much a part of Washington life as the business luncheon in New York or Chicago or the faculty tea on campus. They range all the way from formal receptions with the President entertaining visiting heads of state to the colonel's wife receiving the wives of captains and lieutenants or the bureau chief allowing section hands and their wives to glimpse the splendors of success. The home offices of companies with Washington branches expect their people to make a good impression; so do the home countries of embassies and legations. Parties help.

An ambassador may be more easily persuaded or a Senator convinced over cocktails than in a conference room or an office. A chemist can discuss his work with an engineer, a bureaucrat sympathize with a fellow, or a newsman thrill elegantly gowned women with tales of his adventures. A rising politician may be able to catch the eye of one already risen, or an ambitious civil servant show off the graces of his wife. Sometimes purpose may not be as intense. It may be merely to hear bright gossip, to get a free drink with a smudge of caviar on a wisp of biscuit, or just to break the monotony.

Washington is a graceful and often a gracious place. People are friendly. They speak pleasantly, often with a southern politeness. For the most part, life is gentle in Washington; yet it is not all cakes and ale. There are the usual hazards of American life and some peculiar to the District.

WASHINGTON, D.C.

Traffic is no more murderous in Washington than in any other self-respecting American city, but neither is it less so. Civil servants are not all that civil when they get behind the wheel of a car. The automobile is the great equalizer. A cat is as good as a king, a messenger as good as a bureau chief, a corporal as splendid as a five-star general once he is in his very own driver's seat. When cars are burning in from the residential sections of the city and from the suburbs during the morning rush hours, there is grim purposefulness about Washington driving.

WASHINGTON, D.C.

This is no gay and carefree sport. This is the government on its way to making decisions about war or peace or to mailing out income tax forms or bucking memoranda from one desk to another or just sitting it out until a pension comes due. If you are thinking of crossing an avenue afoot, change your mind. If you want to stop or even slow your car, don't. Washington is filling up. It is just as bad during the late afternoon hours when the government is escaping from itself. Get out of the way.

L'Enfant planned his circles—Scott Circle, DuPont Circle, Chevy Chase Circle, and the others—for sedate carriage traffic, not for drivers who seem intent on qualifying for the Indianapolis Speedway. There is talk of a subway from the suburbs. It might help.

The ordinary pace of Washington is slow partly, perhaps, because the city has a summer every year. Washington steams in summer. People wilt along the streets. Walls of basement rooms show wet spots of dampness, and green and gray mould grows on the shoes on closet floors. The heat banging back from brick and concrete is enervating. It takes an effort of will to move. You gasp when you leave an air-conditioned building and walk into the sun blazing on street or parking lot. For a fraction of an instant you feel you may fall on your face. You don't. You begin to perspire oozily. You become accustomed to the ovenlike atmosphere, and to the humidity that seems thick enough to cut into blocks with a butter knife.

It can get cold in Washington, but not often and not for long. Winter doesn't really mean it in the District. It puts on a show of wet snow occasionally, and then there are days when the damp cold eats into your bones and you feel colder than you might in Maine or Minnesota; but there are not many such days. Winter will end early. It won't be long before the jonquils are out.

Spring makes up quickly and extravagantly for the minor discomforts of the Washington winter. It comes with sudden brilliance and warmth and with rich and varied colorings. Banks of azaleas are in vivid blossom soon after the cherry blossoms have gone. Look at them on the grounds of the old Bureau of Standards out Connecticut Avenue. Beds of tulips in the little parks—there is usually a fine display

The Willard Hotel

Dept of Interior
Simon Bolivar monument

before the Department of the Interior—and about homes are more softly beautiful. It is a southern spring in Washington, caressing and intoxicating.

Washington is Robert E. Lee praying all one night in 1861 in his bedroom at Arlington after he had been offered command of the Union armies at a Blair House meeting that afternoon. It is Julia Ward Howe, after a visit to a nearby Union camp, getting up in her room in the Willard Hotel in the middle of the night to write "The Battle Hymn of the Republic." Abraham Lincoln and his staff had taken refuge in this same Willard at 14th and Pennsylvania when Lincoln slipped unannounced into Washington before his first inaugural.

Washington is the National Shrine of the Immaculate Conception, the largest Roman Catholic church in the United States, at Michigan Avenue and 4th Street, N.E., and almost 500 churches of 60 different faiths. There is even the Washington Mosque, built by 15 Moslem nations.

Executive Office Building (Old State, War and Navy)

It is the old State, War, and Navy Building, wonder of its time, gigantic stone pile on Pennsylvania Avenue next to the White House. Covering four and a half acres, an acre more than the Capitol at that time, it was built of granite blocks of from a quarter ton to 20 tons. It was meant to last a while. It is now the Executive Office Building, the "E.O.B." The ornate structure with its big, high-ceilinged rooms contrasts with the ultramodern John F. Kennedy Center for the Performing Arts, which also is Washington.

The Petersen House where Lincoln died April 15, 1865

The Lincoln Museum

At 10th Street off Pennsylvania is Ford's Theater where Abraham Lincoln was shot. President James A. Garfield was killed by a disappointed office seeker in 1881 at a railroad station which stood where the National Gallery stands now. These, too, are Washington.

Do you know where Nebraska crosses Connecticut and Massachusetts runs into Wisconsin? In Washington, of course. L'Enfant laid out his avenues that way. Only in this city can you step off a sidewalk into England, France, Russia, or India. The buildings and grounds of embassies are considered part of the countries they represent and are not part of American soil or subject to American law.

If this is confusing, the rest of Washington's floor plan is not. Numbered streets run north and south, and though Washington thinks in terms of billions, it counts only to the 60s in its street numbers to the west and to the 30s to the east. Lettered and named streets run east and west in alphabetical order. After the single letters run out, the initial letters of the names indicate position. C Street is farther downtown than M, and Tilden, Upton, and Van Ness much farther out than Belmont.

WASHINGTON, D.C.

Washington is all these things and many more. It is the spaciousness and the greenness and the cleanness and the Congress and the Presidency. It is Watergate concerts by the service bands and orchestras under the stars on the shore of the Potomac, art galleries, Union Station, Dulles Airport, National—but to the people who live there, Washington is a more homely and familiar place. It is the landmarks and conveniences of their own neighborhoods, Hot Shoppe restaurants, Peoples Drug Stores, the *Post* in the morning and the *Star* at night. These are as natural to them as the Washington Monument and the Corcoran Gallery and often more immediately meaningful.

In 1927, a young Mormon from Marriott, Utah, opened a root beer stand at 14th Street and Park Road, N.W. Soon he opened another out Connecticut Avenue. Within two years he had opened three "Hot Shoppe" restaurants. Now there are so many of them throughout the Washington area that the advertisement that says "You are never far from a Hot Shoppe" seems moderate. They are a well-frequented part of the domestic Washington scene.

There is not, but there seems to be, a Peoples Drug Store on every corner, and they are neighborhood institutions. Of course, they sell drugs and the thousands of other items stocked by drugstores, and serve food, ice cream, soft drinks, but they also have bulletin boards. Tacked to these are typed or handwritten notices of rooms for rent, French lessons to be had in exchange for a playpen, or a boy's suit, size 12, for a tuxedo, age 18. You can watch families grow up while you get a bottle of aspirin, buy a magazine, or gulp down a chocolate soda.

Washington has two nationally known newspapers, both thick with news and fat with lucrative advertising. The first issue of the Washington *Post*, the capital's morning newspaper, appeared December 6, 1877, and the paper thrived from the first. Within a year it had a daily circulation of 11,875 and a woman reporter who helped her male fellows cover the city afoot and on a bicycle. The *Post* today has more than fourteen hundred employes and about one hundred reporters. Some four thousand boy carriers deliver it to homes throughout the area.

The Washington *Star*, the city's evening paper, was incorporated

by special act of Congress July 27, 1868, but it had actually been founded 16 years earlier. Like most evening papers, it was started as a medium for local news. In 1853, it had an owner and editor and one "general utility man, assistant editor, reporter and whatnot" at a salary of $12.00 a week. It now has more employes at higher salaries. A conservative sheet, it has yet fought for what it considered needed reforms. Once when the *Star* considered District educational standards too lax, five reporters incorporated themselves as a university and conferred a Doctor of Laws degree on one of the newspaper's copy boys. They proved their point. Housed first in a blacksmith shop, the *Star* moved into a new multimillion-dollar building in 1959. The older Star Building near 11th and Pennsylvania is one of Washington's landmarks.

These are some of the things Washingtonians live with, the familiar institutions of day-to-day life. Like the residents of other cities who often do not bother to see the sights of their own towns, many Washingtonians are aware of the significant monuments and memorials and are glad they are there, but do not let the proximity bother them too much. A hard-working scientist whose government laboratory is far out in the northwestern section of the District said happily that it was eight years since he had gone downtown, and he hoped it would be another eight before he had to again.

Most people have their favorite memories of Washington, and I have mine: of the excitement of watching Presidential election returns in the ballroom of the Sheraton Park (the old Wardman), of noisy inaugural parades, of literally bumping into a famous general as he was trying to get one way through a door and I the other. I once met a Cabinet member informally and was pleased to find him a pleasant gentleman as well as a skilled politician. I met another Cabinet member by appointment and found him as unpleasant as his public utterances had led me to expect. Once I was able to talk for a half hour with a gracious First Lady in the quiet of the President's House.

Other memories have not the glamour of high office about them, but they are as satisfying.

Once I was on a bus going to the Pentagon, which seems bigger

every time you see it. Somehow the driver took a wrong turn on the maze of approaches, and we missed the gargantuan building. We backed up, turned, and tried again. This time we shot by on the other side. On the third try we made it. The driver stopped perspiring, and we all cheered.

I was at Chevy Chase Circle one day when a young woman was trying to park her car. Her small son stood on the back seat encouraging her. "A little more," he said. "A little more. Now turn in."

The right rear wheel hit the curb with a thump and the child was thrown against the back of the front seat with a louder thump. He leaped out and, face contorted with indignation, jumped up and down on the sidewalk shouting, "I knew you'd do it, dammit! I knew you'd do it, dammit!" It was democracy in action; cooperation, then placing the blame squarely where it belonged.

I had gone into a Peoples Drug Store in another part of the city for a cup of coffee. Another small boy climbed up on the stool next to mine, gave the waitress his money, and ordered an ice cream sundae. The waitress made an especially large and luscious one, placed it be-

fore him with a flourish, and said with a smile, "There you are, sonny! Now don't make yourself sick."

Moments later I looked down. The sundae was untouched, and tears were sliding down the small boy's cheeks. I signaled the waitress with a glance, and she came over.

"What's the matter, sonny?"

"Take it away," he said, sobbing, "and bring me one that won't make me sick!"

No moral to the story this time. It is just human. Washington—people there seldom say "Washington"; they say "the District"—is warmly human.

Like other places, the District has its problems. I have not forgotten the indignation of the small children of a freshman Congressman who informed me in council that they had been betrayed. They had helped their father get elected by distributing electioneering pamphlets house-to-house in the far western city where they lived. What no one had properly explained to them was that if he won they would have to leave home and go to Washington. They hated Washington and wanted to go home. They vowed that if their father ran for Congress again they would not help him.

Washington residents had to wait 160 years, until 1961, before they were enfranchised and allowed to vote in Presidential elections. The theory was that in order to protect their jobs they would always vote for the party in power. Evidently that theory has been discarded in favor of a new one.

Further change has been asked. There has been loud and strong demand from some quarters for self-government, its proponents believing that the city should have the right to choose its own officials instead of being run, as it has been since 1874, by a committee of Congress. President Lyndon B. Johnson backed this demand, and the bill giving Washington the right to have its own mayor and city council passed in the Senate. In late September 1965, by a large majority, the House of Representatives voted down the proposal. It passed, instead, a measure that would have citizens of Washington vote on whether or not they want self-government. If their vote shows that they do, they

WASHINGTON, D.C.

would then elect a charter board to draw up a plan for the city's government. This plan would then be submitted to the voters and to both houses of Congress.

After 100 years the White House fence of high iron railings is crumbling in spots and must be replaced. Then there is the matter of the suggested subway.

Like any other community, Washington has always had its problems. Usually they have been solved. Washington came out of struggle of many kinds. As government continues to grow in power, and inevitably in our kind of world it will, Washington will grow with it.

The capable and aggressive go to Washington. A man does not

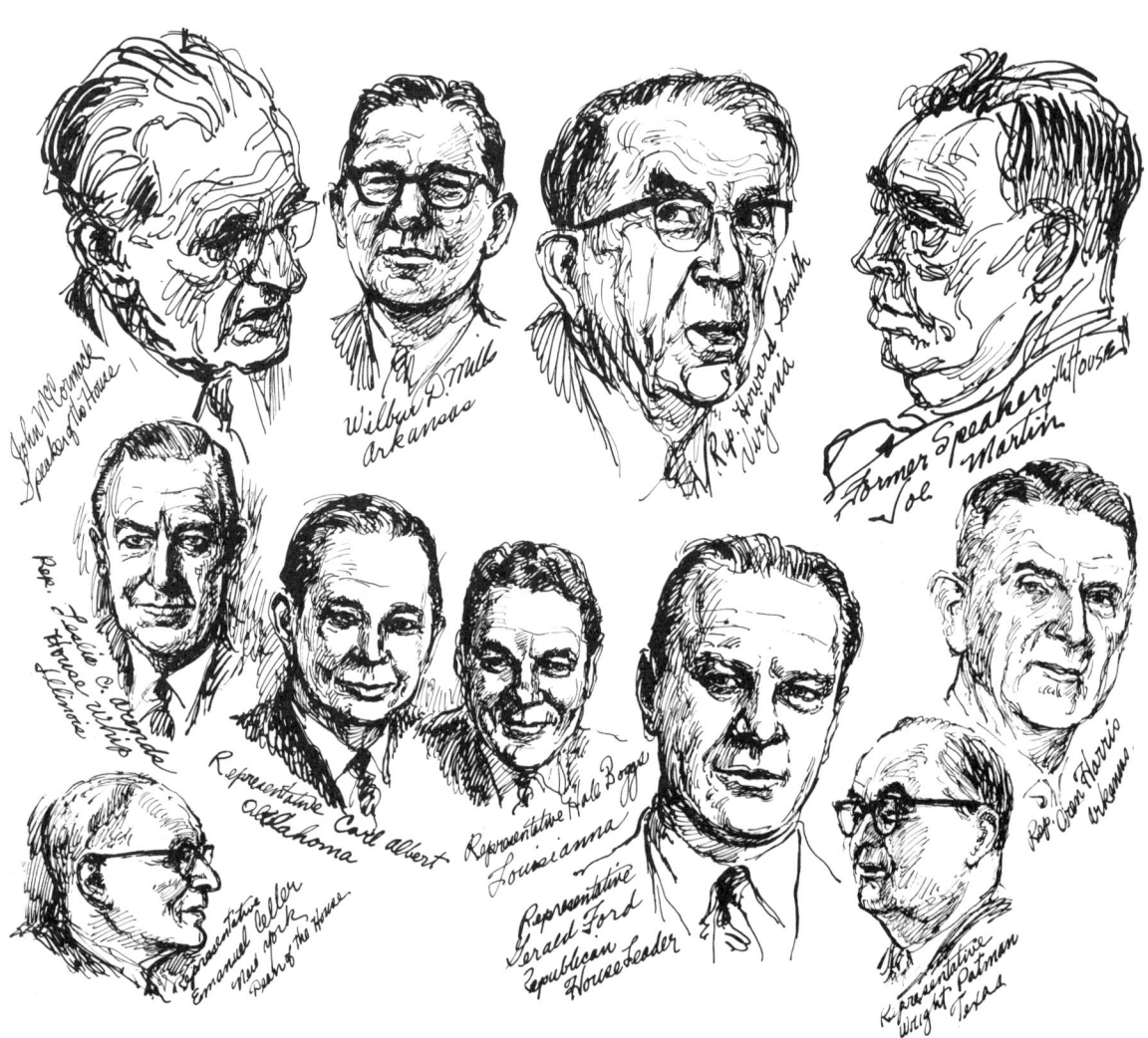

WASHINGTON, D.C.

become successful in public life by an overindulgence in modesty. When the people choose one man over all the others to head the nation, they send him to the White House. When they decide that this man, rather than that man, is the kind of man they want to represent them, they send him to the House or to the Senate. Washington draws

brains and talent, the experts in law, engineering, agriculture, medicine; the specialists in all the arts and sciences with which a whole people are concerned. It attracts the able and the skilled. On its higher nonpolitical levels, Washington's is an elite society.

When the rest of us want to know who we really are, we go to Washington, look at the floodlighted Capitol and the White House and perhaps a few other buildings or at people or just at the graceful city itself, and come away stirred and reassured.

Washington is cosmopolitan, our most cosmopolitan city, yet our most purely American. It talks and talks, and then it acts. It starts out with grand ideas, then gets lost in the details. It can get as confused sometimes as any other city, or as any man or group of men, but it is a more dignified confusion on a grander scale. Yet it is not always confused. It is often very clear. It has to be. When a decision is made to recognize a new country or to add a new state, to send a man to the moon or a submarine to Mars, to drop the most powerful bomb yet, or

WASHINGTON, D.C.

to refrain from dropping any bomb at all, the decision is made in Washington.

Whether the country stands or falls and whether each one of us survives or fails to survive can depend on those decisions. In a way, and in a way that you are sometimes aware of when you are there, Washington is a monument to human trust.